IMPRESSIONS

IMPRESSIONS

SCRIPTURES and DISCUSSION for BIBLE STUDY

EDWARD PORTER ARMSTRONG

McBryde Publishing
NEW BERN NORTH CAROLINA USA

McBryde Publishing
NEW BERN NORTH CAROLINA USA

info@mcbrydepublishing.com.
www.mcbrydepublishing.com

ISBN 978-1-7339824-0-5

McBryde Publishing is a trademark of McBryde Publishing, LLC, New Bern, North Carolina USA

Cover and Interior Layout Designed by Bill Benners

Manufactured in the United States of America

For information regarding special discounts for bulk purchases, Please contact McBryde Publishing Special Sales at 1-252-349-8146 or info@mcbrydepublishing.com

First Paperback Edition June 1, 2019

Table of Contents

About The Author

Ed Armstrong is a native South Carolinian who moved with his parents to North Carolina when he was a teenager. He went to The Citadel for a year and a summer after which he married his High School sweetheart and transferred to Presbyterian Jr. College; from there to High Point University and Duke Divinity School.

Bible was a required course at Presbyterian Jr. College taught by Reverend Dr. Shelton Cosey, a former Flying Tiger in the Pacific during World War II. During his course Ed became captivated by the Biblical message and decided to study for the Christian ministry.

He is presently retired and substitute preaches frequently for fellow ministers. He served as a County Commissioner for twelve years, and on the board of Carolina East Regional Medical Center for twelve years. He is presently an Adjunct Chaplin at the Regional Hospital and a Board Member of Promise Place, a sexual assault resource center.

Ed is an ordained United Methodist Minister. Sarah and Ed have two sons and a daughter.

Preface

I wrote each meditation following private morning devotions and shared them with friends and the Agape Church School Class at Garber United Methodist Church. Some suggested that I publish them. I do so in the manner described by D.T. Niles as "one beggar telling another beggar where to get food." There are no experts on God. These shared thoughts and impressions make no attempt at scholarly historical or textual critical analysis or systematic theological construction. I used the Revised Standard Version and the New Revised Standard Version of the Bible. The verses at the end of each meditation are primarily from The Methodist Hymnal and Cokesbury Worship Hymnal.

The Bible, as the word of God for the people of God, is a several millennia old distilled compilation utilizing a variety of literary styles and compositions influenced by Sacred Presence. It portrays consequences of arrogance and humility before God.

"The wind blows where it wills, and you hear the sound of it, but you do not know whence it comes or whither it goes; so it is with everyone born of the Spirit." (John 3:8)

BEHAVIOR IS THE LANGUAGE OF FAITH!

Words And Other Words
Matthew 6:10-13, King James Version

Our Father .... Life Giver

Who art in heaven .... Where all things originate

Hallowed be thy name .... God alone is good

Thy Kingdom come .... One Master

Thy will be done on earth .... God's desires transform
as it is in heaven.   our desires

Give us this day our daily bread .... God's presence
                                                    nourishes life

And forgive us our trespasses .... Unchain us from a
                                                determined past

As we forgive those who trespass .... Likewise, we unchain
against us   others from a past they
                                                    cannot change

And lead us not into temptation .... Inclinations and influences
                                            we cannot manage

But deliver us from evil A power too great for us to resist alone

For thine is the Kingdom .... Master

And the power.. Control

And the glory .... Good

Forever .... No alternative

Amen .... Let it be so

For my family, friends, and church members who generously endure ministerial narcissism and continue to share their lives with me.

Immanuel

Matthew 1:18-25

Immanuel means "God is with us." Matthew tells us that Jesus is Immanuel. For this reason, it is a never-ending problem for affluent, socially well-positioned, and powerful people to try to clean up Jesus so that he can reside in the proper neighborhood, participate in the better institutions, and get to meet the right people. Jesus' social setback began with his conception in the womb of an unmarried woman. Had his illegitimacy become general knowledge, Mary would have been ridiculed according to the Law; Jesus' first breath was socially unacceptable. From a cultural perspective things went sideways from the outset. However, his mother's betrothed did right by her and followed through with the marriage. After Jesus' death, Matthew and Luke disclosed Joseph's and Mary's secret that the Holy Spirit gave Jesus life, not Joseph. Many devout Christians consider this to be very important. Jesus never referred to this special arrangement in order to get himself out of any binds, elevate his status, or for any other reason. His story was his behavior and His Heavenly Father's endorsement.

"God is with us" didn't cultivate the kind of friends needed to get ahead in this world; one was an extortionist who collected taxes on commission, prostitutes came into the picture from time to time, ritually unclean lepers constituted the bottom of the barrel along with dinner guests referred to as tax collectors and sinners, his disciples lacked the social and religious graces to wash their hands before meals, and they gathered food on the Sabbath. More examples abound in the Bible, but enough is referenced to make the point. In fairness, we should acknowledge a couple of wealthy closet followers who turned out to be exceptions to the low class rule.

I am reminded of what I found when cleaning out my father's storage shed after his death—stacks of crooked boards and cans of bent nails. I remembered what he said when I once asked him why he saved all that old stuff. "I grew up during the great depression of '29 and we didn't throw away anything. Most of the things we built and repaired on the farm were done with crooked boards we sized and bent nails we straightened." The Kingdom of Heaven is populated with crooked and bent souls that God, in his infinite mercy, has made useful.

Contemporary Christians face an awesome test of faith and service as we try to identify people with whom we are comfortable, who are comfortable with Jesus, and who demonstratively need his compassionate and redeeming presence in light of what is reported in the gospels.

Great Father of glory, pure Father of light,
Thine angels adore thee, all veiling their sight;
All praise we would render; O help us to see
Tis only the splendor of light hideth thee.
—*Walter C. Smith*

BEHAVIOR IS THE LANGUAGE OF FAITH!

Not For Everyone
Hebrews 11:32-12:2

Christian religion is not for everyone. Oh, I know what some might say: *"All have sinned and fallen short of the kingdom of God."* However, that's an insider's viewpoint. The world appears generously populated with people who feel good about themselves and seem to function well with family, friends and associates and consider their lives well-managed without Christianity or any formal religion. They exhibit a conventional level of justice and morality and appear free from incapacitating guilt. They manage whatever this earthly life provides and have no interest in any form of afterlife.

"They have their reward." With this in mind, it might be beneficial for Christians to narrow their field of evangelical efforts to those who feel the need for enriched value to earthly life and whatever evolves after death. People who feel empty of purpose and/or burdened with guilt (real or false) tend to be more receptive to the message of divine forgiveness that reorients them toward a more purposeful and productive relationship with God and with those whom they share their time on earth. This is consistent with Jesus teaching that he came, *"not to save the righteous, but the sinner,"* and *"those who are not sick have no need of a physician."*

Some Christians are known to cluster in mutual admiration groups and revel in shared anecdotal accounts of religious experiences that mirror our own. This is habitually followed by Bible studies that concentrate upon the faith of those who lived several thousand years ago. Too frequently, the result is euphoria derived from having a deep and abiding faith in the faith and testimony of others. A parallel might be drawn from the following story.

Leonard was a Methodist preacher and an avid quail hunter. His wife felt the need to frequently remind him that his ministerial responsibilities should be attended to before his bird dog training and quail hunting. It wasn't that he was irresponsible, he just became so engrossed in his training and hunting that occasionally time slipped by before he realized it. This was particularly the case when he sat at Marvin's Country Store and swapped hunting stories with the best bird dog trainers and quail hunters around.

One of the regulars at Marvin's store was Howard. His accounts of memorable quail hunts were among the best. Following one of these story times, Howard told Leonard that he would like to go with him on a hunt. That suited Leonard because he had heard enough to know it would be safe with Howard. He would be going with one of the best. No time was set, but very soon.

Toward the end of the week the preacher called Howard to go on a hunt the next day, or maybe the next, whichever was most convenient. Howard hesitated then awkwardly apologized and declined. His schedule wouldn't permit, but please call again. On three occasions over the next few weeks the preacher attempted to set a convenient time for a hunt. Each time the invitation was declined with regrets.

The preacher was puzzled because the initiative for a hunt always came from Howard. The next day at the post office the preacher saw Gerald, one of the other hunters and storytellers. He told Gerald about the situation with Howard who repeatedly asked to go on a hunt but would always find it inconvenient.

Gerald laughed, "Howard is never going with you hunting. He has never been hunting in his life."

The preacher was flabbergasted. "I have heard Howard tell some of the best hunting stories of anyone in our group."

Gerald replied, "Howard has been sitting with that group for over twenty-five years and all that he knows about hunting is what he has heard from those who are regular hunters. He has just gathered a little bit here and a little bit there from what he heard and made it his own. You are new on the scene and didn't know any better. The rest of us know but we don't ever challenge him because he is an alright guy and we don't want to embarrass him. We let him pretend and we pretend with him."

The preacher could hardly believe what he heard. He told Gerald how Howard had invited him to his house and showed his over-an-under Browning shotgun, his hunting clothes, and a case of gun shells in the bottom of his gun cabinet.

Gerald grinned. "Were his hunting pants worn from going through brush and briars? Was his gunstock nicked and scratched? Did his boots show evidence of walking in the woods?"

The preacher answered, "No."

"That's because he likes to own, show, and talk about high quality hunting paraphernalia. But he's too lazy put it to use. I have seen him wearing hunting clothes while doing yard work and chopping wood, but that's all."

The preacher was out-done, "I never intend to ask him again to go hunting with me, nor will I discuss hunting with him."

Gerald said, "Preacher, I wish you wouldn't do that. And I hope you don't repeat what I told you. Just do like the rest of us; don't hurt his feelings, continue to invite him from time to time, and listen to his stories."

A multitude of people use the Bible like Howard used his hunting stories; they repeat what they read or hear without engaging. *"Jesus called the crowd with his disciples, and said to them, 'If any want to become my followers, let them deny themselves and take up their cross and follow me."* (Mark 8:34)

For those of us who truly feel a devastating sense of guilt, and life without nourishing value and purpose, there is a message of God's forgiveness from Jesus of Nazareth, *"If God is for you, who can be against you?"* The burden is lifted. Beneficiaries can embrace justice, kindness, and humility before God.

> Could my tears forever flow,
> Could my zeal no languor know,
> These for sin could not atone;
> Thou must save and thou alone,
> In my hand no price I bring;
> Simply to thy cross I cling.
> —*Augustus M. Toplady*

BEHAVIOR IS THE LANGUAGE OF FAITH!

Stages And Props
Matthew 23:1-12

Genesis tells us that Adam and Eve hid from God following their disobedience. He called to them and asked why they were hiding. They responded that they recognized their nakedness and were ashamed. With knowledge came the loss of innocence. God responded to their situation by making clothes that hid their nakedness and enabled them to re-socialize. God revealed redemption at the outset.

Jesus corroborated the way emotional and psychological needs relate to garments, titles, and positions when he pointed out that Pharisees and Scribes felt the need to adorn themselves with long fringed head and arm ornaments that flaunted parchments of the Law of Moses. Some of these institutional professionals authenticated their position with costumes, titles, and trappings as they traveled around instructing others in the proper rules for a godly life. Yet, they failed to follow their own detailed instructions. Jesus taught his disciples that the one who is greatest prefers the servant role.

Who needs garments to camouflage guilt more that religious professionals? Who is more aware of "could have, would have, should have" than those who journey inward far enough to feel close kinship with Adam and Eve? Therefore, it is plausible that religious authorities who have sinned enough, repented enough, and been forgiven enough, are authorized to advertise their qualifications to help others address the same condition.

Guilt and shame made Adam and Eve dysfunctional until God provided garments. In like manner, religious professionals who are uncomfortable with only the simple servant role provide themselves various garments, distinguished credentials, auspicious titles, and places of prominence necessary to function effectively. Their need for cover remains because of chronic discomfort with any form of public unveiling.

We should not fail to recognize the similarity between then and now. Religious audiences continue to supply professional actors their stages, costumes, and roles through which listeners vicariously participate in a modified and diminished servant role. Priest, pastor, preacher and parishioner need to be aware of the significance of institutional superfluities that enable those who wear them to come out of hiding to serve God's purpose and during the process learn that, *"all who exalt themselves will be humbled, and all who humble themselves will be exalted."*

> Thou grandest pardon through thy love;
> Thou grace alone availeth.
> Our works could ne'er our guilt remove;
> Yea, e'en the best life failth.
> For none may boast himself of aught,
> But must confess thy grace hath wrought

What-e'er in him is worthy.
—*Martin Luther*

BEHAVIOR IS THE LANGUAGE OF FAITH!

"I Was With You In Weakness"
I Corinthians 2:1-5

Occasionally Christian ministers, priests, preachers, etc are asked what does a "call" to the clergy entail. Paul's explanation in his letter to the Corinthians is concise. However, it isn't the response to which most people can easily relate. Perhaps this tale I composed about Sam the signal man might be helpful.

When Sam entered the tenth grade he was eligible to try out for the varsity football team. He knew he did not have physical attributes or player skills as most of the other guys, but he wanted to give it a try. He had friends trying out and he was comfortable being with them.

Sam barely made the first cut at the tryouts. Yet, he was pleased to be there. He made it through the conditioning drills and was issued a uniform. Reality set in when the coach began assigning positions. The best athletes were picked for the first team. Then the second team was named, followed by Sam and another aspirant who were left unassigned.

Sam was not surprised, but he was a little embarrassed and disappointed. The other boy walked into the dressing room, turned in his uniform, took a shower, and went home. Sam had no intentions of quitting. He was on the team and there he intended to stay unless unwanted. Day after day the practice teams took the field to hone their skills as Sam, in full gear, watched.

The cheerleaders were practicing on the sidelines with routines they would demonstrate during games. Sam's eyes were regularly drawn to a cheerleader who was in his sophomore class. She saw him looking and smiled her approval. From time to time he sauntered over to where she was and engaged in small talk.

They were chatting one afternoon while the cheerleaders were taking a break and he heard the Coach's voice bellow out, "Sam, come here. I don't need anyone to entertain cheerleaders." Sam's face reddened because the ballplayers turned to see what aroused the coach. Sam grabbed his headgear and ran to the coaches' side for assignment and instructions.

The coach put his arm around him and said, "Sam, one of the most important positions on this team is held by the person who walks next to me along the sidelines during every game, and uses prearranged hand signals that I give him to convey the offensive and defensive sets to the players on the field. Each set has a number and when I call the number out your assignment is to immediately send the appropriate hand signal to the players of the field. Will you do that?"

Sam was thrilled beyond words. He stammered, "Yes coach." Sam liked being close to the coaches. He liked knowing all those signals and being able to actually control what was happening on the field even though he was a pass-through. He would walk step for step with the man in control and he was in full view of everyone on the field and in the stands who knew that his position was necessary.

Sam's primary concern was that he accurately conveys the proper signal from the coach. Otherwise, his players would be out of place. What followed could lead to defeat. Whether Sam's team won or lost, his performance evaluation was entirely based upon the accuracy with which he transmitted the coaches' signals to the players on the field. Sam was never involved in post-game interviews by the school paper because his job description rendered personal pronouns and personal references inappropriate.

Sam, like the Apostle Paul, and all effective signal-persons who have answered the call, was able to say *"my speech and my message were not in plausible words of wisdom, but in demonstration of the Spirit and power."*

To serve the present age,
My calling to fulfill;
O may it all my powers engage
To do my Master's will.
—*Charles Wesley*

Perishable And Tested

I Peter 1:3-9

Christians *"live in hope"* with *"faith in the resurrection of Jesus Christ"* that is *"perishable"* and is *"tested."* What a way to daily face a materialistic world that asks straightforward, "Where's the meat?" The least effective reaction is a plethora of scriptural quotations presented as objectively-verified facts.

What is more effective? Follow the example of Jesus whose words and deeds established what he believed. The word made flesh is the only mechanism for authentication available to Christians. God's revelation through Jesus was an act of confrontation and conflict between the world of power and control and the Kingdom of God wherein humble service is primary.

Christians *"live in hope"* because formless void never concedes to humble service. Every day, and in every way, power and control are manifested in personal and institutional undertakings. Believers who are wise take to heart the warning of the Apostle Paul, *"So I find it to be a law that when I want to do what is good, evil lies close at hand."* Satan disguises himself as an angel of light. The hope in which Christians live is grounded in God's presence authenticated by guidance and energy that enables one to serve. Faith is *"perishable"* and it is *"tested."* For this reason, we look for nourishment from the Giver of Life who alone can empower.

Paul's instructions to the church at Philippi cannot be misunderstood. *"Do nothing from selfish ambition or conceit, but in humility regard others as better than yourselves. Let each of you look not to your own interests, but to the interests of others. Let the same mind be in you that was in Christ Jesus..."* So, as Christians we are asked to manage our earthly existence based upon faith in God's resurrection of a man who was crucified for a life of service that ran counter to prevailing opportunities for success. Although we "Love to Tell the Story" and lift up the precious name of Jesus, we will be tested when our servant role is disconcerting to *"earthly powers."*

Intellect Is No Substitute For Faith
Acts 17:16-34

Intellect is no substitute for faith. Thankfully intellect is utilized by faith. Faith is described in the book of Hebrews as *"the assurance of things hoped for and the conviction of things unseen."* This allows for divine influence without claiming objective verifiable knowledge about God. The existence of multiple religions implies a universal sense of Sacred Presence. Through art and imagination, people have always utilized the best available information and material to express their feelings about spiritual awareness. However, Paul warns that God is a universal presence Who cannot be captured by intellect, imagination, or any quantifiable concept.

The author of Ecclesiastes offered this common sense observation: *"He has made everything suitable for its time; moreover He has put a sense of past and future in their minds, yet they cannot find out what God has done from the beginning to the end."* It is in this context that Paul considers it reassuring to refer to God as one *"Who is not far from each one of us."*

After giving due credit to past accomplishments amid understandable limitations, Paul says it is now time to be more mature because God, through the introduction of a new character (Jesus), reveals all that is needed to get a sense of what went on at the beginning as well as the direction things will take as the creation moves toward conclusion. As struggling actors, we are free to improvise our parts as the plot develops. But the last scene is fixed.

Paul proceeded to legitimize his message by announcing Jesus' resurrection from the dead to an audience who had not heard of it. For the most part they considered it silly because objective proof was not (nor is it currently) available. Paul confidently believed that God's presence alone verifies his message. Since *"His presence is not far from any of us...,"* our understanding is relationship-dependent. There are some who view all of the above as nothing more than an example of a universal neurosis.

It was not in the wind, or the earthquake, or the fire that the prophet Elijah heard God. Rather, it was in sheer silence that *"the voice came to him."* Elijah's spiritual experience affected his life. In the same way, the resurrection of Jesus, coupled with the influential presence of God, gains a hearing because of changes in the believer's life. This is the only authentication available. *"Be doers of the word and not merely hearers who deceive themselves. For if any are hearers of the word and not doers, they are like those who look at themselves in a mirror, for they look at themselves and, on going away, immediately forget what they look like."* (James 1:23)

> Open my eyes that I may see
> Glimpses of truth thou hast for me;
> Place in my hands the wonderful key
> That shall unclasp and set me free.
> Silently now I wait for thee,
> Ready my God thy will to see;
> Open my eyes, illumine me, Spirit divine.
> —Clara H. Scott

BEHAVIOR IS THE LANGUAGE OF FAITH!

Arrangements
Colossians 4:2-17

"*The mystery of Christ*" is the basis for community witness. Mysteries by definition provide little, if any, objectively verified support for what is involved. Paul wrote the Colossian letter while he was in prison. He asked the church to offer prayers of thanksgiving and prayers that **"God will open for us a door for the word...so that I may reveal it clearly, as I should."**

There appears to be no doubt in the mind of Paul that God is the one who utilizes the best witness one can offer in order to give maximum opportunity for the hearer to respond to the **"mystery of Christ."** Believers are not called upon to provide a powerful convincing argument that overcomes all resistance. Jesus emphasized the servant role as the means of declaring his Lordship. Maintaining the servant theme, Paul counseled the church to **"let your speech always be gracious..."**

Power supplies the primary exchange for earthly transactions, and whatever is gained by means of earthly power is loss for God's suffering servant. History records an unimaginable degree of destruction and human suffering done in the name of religion when it attempts to use power and control over temporal things in an effort to promote and enhance that which is eternal. When we "render unto Caesar the things that are Caesar's...," **"we need to recognize what we are doing; we need not expect anything to come of it beyond the managed results expected from 'principalities and powers'."**

"No one serves two masters." The master whom Christians serve is the one from whom we accept the description of life's highest and best use. In contrast, we have Satan, the master of instant gratification who specializes in fulfillment of earthly desires. We read how he operates when testing Jesus (Matthew 4:1-11), who summarized their conflict, **"Worship the Lord your God, and serve him only."**

Serving God is described in I John 3:14-24: **"We know that we have passed from death to life because we love one** *another... How does God's love abide in anyone who has the world's goods and sees a brother or sister in need and yet refuses to help? Little children, let us not love in word or speech, but in truth and action...and by this we know that he abides in us, by the Spirit that he has given us."*

O Love that will not let me go,
I rest my weary soul in thee;
I give thee back the life I owe,
That in thine ocean depths its flow
May richer, fuller be.
—*George Matheson*

BEHAVIOR IS THE LANGUAGE OF FAITH!

Which Gate
II Thessalonians 2:1-12

E vil motivates people to act contrary to self-interest by instigating what the Bible considers rebellion against the Creator. Biblical laws are tutorials designed to impede evil and to promote behavior that honors the Creator.

The Bible presents the ***"power of God"*** and the "power of Satan as competing powers in the universe." Both are greater than human power. There are those who de-emphasize the authenticity of competing powers—they prefer to rely upon unencumbered freewill. Christians should be cautious about this. Paul warns in his letter to the Ephesians, ***"For our struggle is not against enemies of blood and flesh, but against the rulers, against the authorities, against the cosmic powers of the present darkness, against the spiritual forces of evil in the heavenly places."*** Apparently, it is a major conflict into which humans are born.

Paul counseled the Thessalonian church that evil's deceptive practices are primarily directed toward people who are in distress and vulnerable. They are more easily persuaded to replace Biblical laws (or other religious codes) with behavior that centers upon personal gratification. He teaches that it is delusional to think and act as though pleasure can ultimately result from ungodly and destructive behavior that is unconcerned with how others are affected.

Jesus observed that godly behavior requires considerable effort: *"Enter through the narrow gate; for the gate is wide and the road is easy that leads to destruction, and there are many who take it. For the gate is narrow and the road is hard that leads to life, and there are few who find it."*

God enables humanity to choose the gate, the path, and the way by which others are influenced. No power on earth can expunge word and deed once they are done. Therefore, every moment requires commitment to get it right the first time. The Psalmist announced, *"Happy are those who do not follow the advice of the wicked, or take the paths that sinners tread, or sit in the seat of scoffers; but their delight is in the Law of the Lord, and on his Law they meditate day and night."*

Paul was a student of the Laws of Moses. Yet, he admitted frustration with obedience to the Law. *"So I find it to be a law that when I want to do what is good, evil lies close at hand. For I delight in the Law of God in my inmost self, but I see in my members another law at war with the war of my mind, making me captive to the law of sin that dwells in my members. Wretched man that I am! Who will rescue me from this body of death? Thanks be to God through Jesus Christ our Lord."* Correspondingly, Christians pray, *"...for thine is the kingdom, and the power, and the glory forever. Amen."*

> We by his spirit prove
> And know the things of God,
> The things which freely of his love
> He hath on us bestowed.
> —*Charles Wesley*

BEHAVIOR IS THE LANGUAGE OF FAITH!

Truth
John 18:33-38

At the conclusion of his interrogation, Pilate asked Jesus, *"What is the truth?"* The answer to his question was standing before him. Pilate was "hard wired" to understand truth as political power. Jesus exemplified divine power. The Bible repeatedly illustrates how *"hardness of heart"* shapes human decisions. Hurting others means nothing. *"Hardness of heart"* is a primitive description for inner feelings that are basically unalterable. In Pilate's case, he was predisposed (hardness of heart) to evaluate life in terms of power and there was no criminal accusation or activity, no army of insurrection, nor any violations as a basis for passing judgment. So, he asked Jesus, *"What have you done?"*

Jesus' reply defined the problem. *"My kingdom is not from this world."* Christians are better informed than Pilate about the kingship of Jesus who lived the truth he described. *"The greatest among you will be your servant. All who exalt themselves will be humbled, and all who humble themselves will be exalted."*

Modern experiments in ornithology determined that songbirds raised in isolation during early development are never able to sing, even when later placed permanently with singing birds. Terms such as "hard wired", "hardness of heart", and "forever the child" express recognition of a similar degree of permanency in living organisms that requires tenacious effort to manage. Jesus said, *"Truly I tell you, whoever does not receive the kingdom of God as a little child will never enter it."* Believers must bypass the old connections and as little children form new ones. Paul's advice gave comfort and encouragement to the Christian community in Philippi; *"Beloved, I do not consider that I have made it my own, but this one thing I do: forgetting what lies behind and straining forward to what lies ahead, I press on toward the goal for the prize of the heavenly call of God in Jesus Christ."* The songbird never sang, but it enhanced knowledge and was beautiful to see as it flitted about among the singing birds. By God's grace, we manage who we are and work out who we shall be.

I find, I walk, I love, but oh, the whole
Of love is but my answer, Lord, to thee!
For thou wert long beforehand with my soul;
Always thou lovedst me.
—*The Pilgrim Hymnal*

BEHAVIOR IS THE LANGUAGE OF FAITH!

No Answer
Psalm 88

Who can provide an answer to God's lack of response to the psalmist's desperate plea, **"O Lord, why do you cast me off? Why do you hide your face from me?"** This tormented man further declares that his **"soul is full of troubles"** and his health had been **"wretched and close to death from my youth up."** Every morning **"my prayer comes before you."** Yet, he says, **I am shut in so that I cannot escape.** There is no recorded response from God. Believers are left to think and rationalize. Psalm 88 is a poetic presentation of a lamentable situation.

In the same vein, the book of Job consists of forty-one chapters of discourse between Job, his three neighbors, and God addressing the issue of why a faithful man like Job experiences disaster while scoundrels "trip the light fantastic" across life's glorious stage. Job expresses his unhappiness with God's inequity. His friends accuse him of deception. God chastises him for arrogance. His issue is not addressed. Centuries later an anonymous rabbi didn't like the gloomy ending so he attempted to mitigate previous chapters by adding the Cinderella chapter 42 which attempts to gloss over the absence of a clear answer.

Jesus was on the cross when he quoted from Psalm 22:1, *"My God, my God, why hast Thou forsaken me?"* Jesus, like Job, felt abandoned. There is no recorded answer from God. The cry from Jesus appears reasonable. God has humanity on a "needs to know" status. By faith we are confident that He controls and is just. *"The wind blows where it chooses, and you hear the sound of it, but you do not know where it comes from or where it goes. So it is with everyone who is born of the Spirit."* Jesus said the Spirit would not leave us comfortless.

We are called upon to *"pray without ceasing"* and heed the words of Jesus, *"Father into thy hands I commend my spirit."* We live by a sense of God's presence rather than by analysis of His mind. We are called to respond as He inclines our hearts. Objective knowledge is limited to what we discover in creation. Be thankful there are no experts on God; only witnesses to the presence of One Who is **continuously aware** of our needs and the **appropriate support response** when we cry for help.

I thank thee more that all our joy
Is touched with pain;
That shadows fall on brightest hours,
That thorns remain;
So that earth's bliss may be our guide,
And not our chain.
—*Adelaide A. Procter*

BEHAVIOR IS THE LANGUAGE OF FAITH!

Intimacy
Psalm 77

This ancient poet's cry to God in time of trouble ends without the desired response. He wonders why. Although the Psalm doesn't lay out an answer in plain view, there might be a hint in the writer's references to past events. He seeks God's help because of trouble and he wants comfort for his troubled heart. His search for relief leads him to meditate upon God's mighty works done years ago. This focus upon the past might be an indication of why he feels so disconnected from God concerning his immediate difficulties. He is obviously impressed with God's power and mighty works seen in thunder, whirlwinds, lightning, earthquakes, and deliverance in the past.

What is missing is any history of his daily quiet time with God, Who shows an interest in personal things and with Whom he shares small talk. Such intimate awareness of God's presence enables routine consultation rather than a call out of obscurity to do mighty works. It might be that mighty works of wonder are less frequently needed when concerns, great and small, are addressed daily before they become bewildering and unmanageable. The Bible teaches us about intimacy with God and provides us with an unmistakable image: **"Listen! I am at the door knocking; if you hear my voice and open the door I will come in to you and eat with you and you with me."**

I recall a very moving account given by Dr. Hugh Anderson during one of his class lectures which I attended at Duke Divinity School. Dr. Anderson was from Scotland and was a young man living in London during World War II. He told of the horror of living through the daily bombing raids and how he found comfort and reassurance in the intimate presence of God who was down where the bombs were falling. With emotion he said, "There would have been no purpose for, or benefit from, a God who dwelt out beyond the stars."

Paul's words to the church in Rome covers all the bases by saying, *"For I am convinced that neither death, nor life, nor angels, nor rulers, nor things present, nor things to come, nor powers, nor height, nor depth, nor anything else in all creation, will be able to separate us from the love of God in Christ Jesus our Lord."*

> O Joy that seekest me through pain,
> I cannot close my heart to thee;
> I trace the rainbow through the rain
> And feel the promise is not vain
> That morn shall tearless be.
> —*George Matheson*

BEHAVIOR IS THE LANGUAGE OF FAITH!

Verification
Isaiah 7:10-16

Biblical writers regard the Creator of the universe to be immortal. *"In the beginning God..."* are words of faith upon which all that follows is predicated. The question arises as to how the Immortal Creator makes Himself known to mortals. There is never a shortage of mortals who say they speak on behalf of the Creator. This makes it necessary for those who have an interest in divine communication to devise some standard of verification that the Creator has communicated.

What is the sign verifying Divine communication? Isaiah says the immortal shall put on mortality and will be called Immanuel (God with us). Practically speaking, should any other method be expected? Words vary in meaning and are subject to misunderstanding. Words are made to describe things created and are inadequate to define anyone (God and citizens of heaven) or anything else (eternity) that is not created. Relying upon words for divine verification lends itself to human arrogance and control.

Isaiah predicted that the Creator will be known through people-to-people contact. Deeds will fulfill *"the demand for a sign."* The Christian message to the world is that Jesus of Nazareth is the mortal sign of Immortal presence and purpose. To the point, Jesus said: *"All things have been handed over to me by my Father, and no one knows the Son except the Father, and no one knows the Father except the Son and anyone to whom the Son chooses to reveal him."*

"Demand for a sign" is evident in behavior in spite of human weakness and imperfection. The words *"demand for a sign"* bring to mind a story told by Jack Martin from Greenwood Mississippi; also, my friend and roommate at Duke Divinity School; and a United Methodist Church minister in the 1960s on a multi-church circuit in Alaska. One of the churches Jack served was in a small isolated community that was accessible in winter only by plane—the landing strip was a frozen lake. Jack and his wife Rachel (a registered nurse) would fly in on Friday, visit with the membership for the weekend, preach on Sunday, and fly out on Monday. Their living quarters was one room in the church attic which was equipped with a wood heater, a small two burner gas cook-stove, two chairs, and a bed.

This particular Sunday morning greeted them with the results of a heavy snow during the night. Everything was buried in snow, unusual only because it was an exceptionally heavy accumulation, even for that community. Rachel remarked that she doubted anyone would even try to attend services. Jack, the optimist, continued to prepare for morning services by building a fire in the big wood heater that sat in the center of the church. It didn't make it warm enough to remove outer clothing. It was barely better than nothing.

At five minutes 'till eleven, Rachel said, "Jack, no one's coming; we may as well close the damper, let the fire die down, and go back to our cozy little room. Jack said, "No" and told Rachel to stand for the invocation. "It's Sunday; Jesus said *'Where two or more are gathered in my name, I am there also'.*" As Jack tells it, he and Rachel had just finished singing "I Love To Tell The Story" when the church door opened and one man walked in and sat down. Jack knew the man, although, not very well. He lived alone about five miles from the church on a gold mining claim that he worked since coming to

Alaska during the 1930s depression. His small claim never made him wealthy. However, it produced enough for him to live. He had no other family.

Jack preached to his congregation of two. At the conclusion of the sermon Jack announced the closing hymn, extended the invitation to come for prayer at the communion rail, and, if so inclined, to make a profession of faith. As the three of them sang, the old miner walked down the aisle and told Jack he wanted to be baptized and join the church. That was on his mind when he got up that morning and decided to walk to church regardless of the foul weather. The vows of baptism and church membership were made then and there. God is with us!

BEHAVIOR IS THE LANGUAGE OF FAITH!

No Room For Evil
Ephesians 4:25-32

One of the first things we learned in seventh grade science was the basic law of physics that "two objects cannot occupy the same space at the same time." I don't recall that my life was dramatically affected by this knowledge. Yet, it is important because it sets the stage for understanding that we live in a deterministic environment of objects which shift around but remain within what the ancients referred to as *"...the dome that separated the waters under the dome from the waters that were above the dome..."* Primitive analysis, yet, we get the picture. Science can discover, analyze, and play with the toys that are given, but it must adhere to the rules and nothing can be removed from the room.

Paul writes to the Ephesians and sends a message that is similar to the law of physics concerning objects: *"Do not make room for the devil."* Ah! Creative and redemptive good cannot occupy the same space at the same time with destructive evil. The dissimilarity is that physics laws are deterministic, but issues concerning good and evil involve choice. Paul doesn't imply choices, but choice. Thereafter, good or evil appear to exercise their respective powers within the space provided. These powers can operate in whatever dimensions we **"make room."**

Jesus offered this wisdom saying: *"When the unclean spirit has gone out of a person, it wanders through waterless regions looking for a resting place, but it finds none. Then it says 'I will return from my house from which I came.' When it comes, it finds it empty, swept, and put in order. Then it goes and brings along seven other spirits more evil than itself, and they enter and live there; and the last state of that person is worse than the first."*

Paul says *"make room"* for the creative and redemptive power of good which is expressed in *"being kind to one another, tenderhearted, forgiving one another, as God in Christ has forgiven you."* No complex theology, just a message as simple and clear as a basic law of physics.

An Example
John 14:6

Jesus said, *"I am the way, the truth, and the life..."* His earthly life defined what this means and was generally rejected by the masses, the religious establishment, and the government that killed him. This rejected life and message focused upon humility before God and a relationship with others that he described as *"Whoever wishes to be great among you must be your servant, and whoever wishes to be first among you must be your slave... So, if I, your Lord and Teacher, have washed your feet, you ought also to wash one another's feet. For I have set you an example, that you also should do as I have done to you. Very truly, I tell you, servants are not greater than their master nor are messengers greater than the one who sent them."*

Life begins when multiple sperm aggressively and powerfully strive through the female reproductive system to be the one that fertilizes a receptive egg and forms an embryo. There is no evidence that the weakest and least aggressive sperm is, at the moment before fertilization, supernaturally catapulted to the front of the mass in order to complete a humble process. However, throughout the creative process, human life develops awareness of an influential presence that elevates life's meaning and purpose beyond basic aggression and power. The ancients pictured humanity's awareness of this enhancement as: ***"Then the Lord God formed man from the dust of the ground and breathed into his nostrils the breath of life; and the man became a living being (in the Creator's likeness)."*** This final act of creation raises the bar and gives humans enhanced management responsibility to ***"have dominion over"*** and ***"subdue"*** the natural order in a manner that reflects the creator's influence. Genesis presents a powerful image of the Creator and those He created strolling about in the cool of the evening enjoying an idyllic environment. This is disrupted when humankind opted to manage on its own and exercise unilateral control like the Creator.

Sam was a twelve-year-old city boy who looked forward to summer visits on Uncle Bill's farm. Bill was the only one of Sam's mother's siblings who remained on the farm after graduating from Farm Life High School. Uncle Bill and his wife, Aunt Carrie, had no children. They adored Sam's visits and planned ahead to make sure he relished every day.

Uncle Bill was an avid bear hunter with the reputation of being one of the best dog trainers in the county. He always had a litter of pups around from which he picked what he considered to be the best hunting prospects. The remainder of the litter he sold or gave away.

One of Sam's favorite things was sitting in the yard swing and watching Uncle Bill perform training exercises. The training for this particular day was designed to encourage the seven-month-old dogs to aggressively track and pursue a bear through the woods. The training technique required that a long rope be attached to tanned bear hide and then dragged around in the yard in front of the dogs so they could grab it in their teeth and shake it. This provided a vague approximation that allowed the dogs to identify their game during a live bear hunt.

When Uncle Bill stopped for a rest, Sam offered a suggestion; wouldn't it be better training if I wrapped myself in the bear rug and rolled around in the dirt where the dogs could see me? You hold them so they can't get me. I will run down that cotton row toward the big oak tree at the end of the row and just before I get to the tree, you turn the dogs loose. I'll climb the tree before they get to me. That will be just like a real bear chase. Uncle Bill grinned at his twelve-year-old big city nephew and said, "We'll give it a try."

Everything proceeded just as Sam described. When Sam was half-way to the oak tree he waived for Uncle Bill to turn the dogs loose. Those three young hounds raced down the cotton row faster than Sam imagined. They caught up with him just as he got to the base of the tree. Their teeth latched onto the bear rug just like they did when it wasn't wrapped around Sam. The difference was they latched on to a little bit of bear rug and a little bit of Sam at the same time. Sam was sufficiently covered so that no skin was broken, but the pinch was more than he wanted. Sam began to squall, "Uncle Bill, Uncle Bill, help me!" Uncle Bill knew Sam was in no danger. None-the-less, he trotted toward the unintended conclusion of Sam's training program, laughing and shouting mockingly, "stand it if you can Sam, it'll be the making of the pups."

Like Sam, we can rely upon our limited time and experience and choose our own training program for life—one that rewards self-centeredness, power, oppression, and greed, or, we can defer to the eternal training program described by the apostle Paul as *"love, joy, peace, patience, kindness, generosity, faithfulness, gentleness, and self-control."*

The options might appear initially to be a no-brainer. However, a testing program has been in place from the beginning of human awareness wherein the tester makes an elaborate appeal to personal gratification by down-playing human limitations. God's tutorial program, like Uncle Bill's, allows for unintended consequences that are specifically designed to encourage humility in the presence of superior knowledge and authority.

"...work out your own salvation with fear and trembling;
for it is God who is at work in you, enabling you both
to will and to work for His good pleasure."
—Philippians 2:12-13

BEHAVIOR IS THE LANGUAGE OF FAITH!

The Image
Isaiah 6:1-8

I saiah presents a beautiful word-picture as he describes his personal worship experience in the Temple. Heavenly beings surround God glorifying His beauty and holiness. During this intense worship, the prophet becomes acutely aware of his imperfections and unworthiness. He pictures God's response as an angel touching his lips with a hot coal that burns away his imperfections and makes him feel accepted in the presence of perfection.

The verbal image presented by Isaiah is not the work of an amateur. It masterfully expresses deep emotions developed over a time of struggle with imperfections from which we can learn, as do art students who spend quality time with the creative paintings of master artists as an important learning and talent evaluation tool, without which they are restricted to an artless life of imitative painting. In a similar manner, Christians see in Jesus God's masterful embodiment of spiritual maturity by which we evaluate our personal and communal spiritual development. Otherwise, we are restricted to a life of imitative faith limited to recitations of memorable faith events about which we have read or heard in the lives of others.

We can but stand in awe at the thought of God's perfection. It presents no challenge. In contrast, our lives are defined by our struggle with the imperfections that we choose to protect, nurture, and blend into our self-portrait without regard for their effect on others. We should develop fruits of the Spirit to replace them. We repent and call upon God to forgive us and to touch our lips with a burning coal that will make pure what our efforts cannot. Only then do we have an experience-based story that God can send us out to tell.

Let not conscience make you linger,
Nor of fitness fondly dream;
All the fitness He requireth
Is to feel your need of Him.
This He gives you, This He gives you,
'Tis the Spirit's glimmering beam.
—*Joseph Hart*

Falling In Love With Love
John 1:35-51

"Falling in love with love is playing with make-believe" is a line from a 50s golden oldie. No mistaking the message about fickle romance. There is a parallel message for Christian pilgrims on a journey of faith. Faith in the faith of others can also be make-believe. Vicarious or secondhand faith can result when Bible study and devotional exercises form the core of one's spiritual experience.

God awareness might be compared to romance because both have been around "since the memory of mankind runneth not to the contrary," and both have experienced considerable deception. I often refer to Ecclesiastes 3:11 as reference to humanity's frustration over incomplete understanding of God because redundancy is appropriate for emphasizing that *"...God has put a sense of past and future in their minds, yet they cannot find out what God has done from the beginning to the end."*

This leads us to journey within ourselves and develop a sense of divine presence and direction, or satisfy our spiritual yearnings with conversation and study about impressive people of faith who displayed admirable qualities and did worthy things as a result of their inward journey and outward manifestations of a relationship with God. In other words, Christian faith is not theater, except when it inappropriately approximates shadow dancing.

When we develop our spiritual life solely upon knowledge and recitation of what others of faith have said and done, this too is make-believe. Faith is viable when we do something because we experience the influence of Sacred Presence. In this way our faith builds an experience base that in turn makes the faith of others a shared experience that is meaningful to hear and read about.

God is in our life. Yet, our knowledge and experience is limited, or broadened, by His involvement in moment-by-moment joint ventures. This is not make-believe. Rather, it makes a difference. For this reason, a community of Christians was brought before government authorities in Thessalonica shouting the accusation, *"These people who have been turning the world upside down have come here also."*

"In The Beginning..."
Genesis 1 & John 1

"*In the beginning God created...*" is a declaration of faith —"*the assurance of things hoped for and the conviction of things unseen*"—not a declaration of fact (generally known and objectively verified). The Biblical message is that all existence is a gift not an entitlement. Never mind that the equity issue is incomprehensible. The perception remains that existence as we experience it, more or less, for better or worse, did not originate from the effort of any material being within oral or recorded history. It is a gift.

The delivery mechanism was the spoken word of God, Who said what was to be done and it was accomplished. The Word reported to God after each project and God specifically said that it was good, which means it was done the way He wanted it and it functioned according to His purpose.

The creation of humanity was different in that it was a joint venture involving the Creator and others who were present. Humans were created in the image of the Creator, Who, oddly enough, did not pronounce them as good. That could mean something significant, or it might have been an oversight or nothing more than a senior moment. Nonetheless, five mechanistic things were called good, and the sixth was given management responsibility but no prefatory evaluation. It makes sense that the Creator would want to hold off until He could see how it worked out.

The Bible reports that our ancestors didn't get it together and totally blew a great arrangement. The opening verses of the Gospel of John tell that the Word that did all of the real grunt work during creation returned to the scene, this time in the flesh, in Jesus. The purpose of this arrangement was, and continues to be, a demonstration of the purpose and method of the Creator's management plan which He intended from the beginning. The Apostle Paul shares John's point of view when he refers to Jesus as the second Adam. There was no question about the need to start over because the mess was beyond fixing.

In order to make the new deal doable, Jesus proposed a two-step arrangement that would begin human realignment with the presence and purpose of the Creator and discontinue the current program that wasn't working. The Creator forgives all that has gone before. He provides help overcoming and overriding what is hardwired from the past and empowers rewiring for the present and future as embodied in Jesus. All this is done with patience and understanding as mortals repent and *work out our salvation with fear and trembling for it is God who is at work in you...*

Father, I stretch my hands to Thee;
No other help I know;
If Thou withdraw Thyself from me,
Ah! Whither shall I go?
What did Thine only Son endure,
Before I drew my breath!
What pain, what labor, to secure
My soul from endless death!
Surely Thou canst not let me die;
O speak, and I shall live;
And here I will unwearied lie,
Till Thou Thy Spirit give. Author of faith!
To Thee I lift my weary longing eyes;
O let me now receive that gift!
My soul without it dies.
—*Charles Wesley*

BEHAVIOR IS THE LANGUAGE OF FAITH!

Angel Message
Acts 27:21-26

Throughout his Christian life, the Apostle Paul remained focused upon his commitment to share Jesus' message of forgiveness and redemption with Gentiles. His conviction was demonstrated during a storm at sea when he was on his way to carry out an appeal to the emperor for a judicial hearing on the accusation of sedition against Rome. He was convinced that God would see him through regardless of impediments.

The crew and passengers were fortunate to have someone on board who was convinced of divine assurance that their journey would be completed safely regardless of being run aground by a storm. Like most people, they had never interacted with an angel. So, it is understandable that this extraordinary aspect of Paul's account would become a focal point. This is unfortunate because the primary feature of this account is Paul's commitment to carry out his mission to the Gentiles.

Reason tells us that the angel used a very inconvenient method to accomplish the purpose. Why not just calm the storm, clear the skies, and send a strong favorable wind to hasten the day when Paul would have his moment before the emperor? Such a logical and factual analysis is to miss the message and the mystery that in spite of storm, shipwreck, and lengthy delay, Paul's mission to the Gentiles would be accomplished. Obviously, divine purpose doesn't recognize any necessity to make time and circumstance convenient. If hardships tend to exacerbate doubt, then faith can either strengthen and deepen or wilt and melt.

If, on a quiet sea,
Toward heaven we calmly sail,
With grateful hearts,
O God, to Thee,
We'll own the favoring gale.
But should the surges rise,
And rest delay to come,
Blest be the tempest, kind the storm,

Which drives us nearer home.
Soon shall our doubts and fears
All yield to Thy control;
—*Augustus M. Toplady*

Fasting And Seeing
Exodus 3:13-15; Isaiah 58:3-9; Luke 22:27

The purpose and efficacy of fasting came up in a recent group discussion on religious rituals and practices. The fifty-eighth chapter of Isaiah asserts that religious fasting and rituals change nothing in a social setting where people are in *"the bonds of injustice... and the yolk of oppression ...where people are hungry, homeless, and without clothes."* Only when these issues are addressed can anyone be enlightened, healed, vindicated, and God glorified; only then will He say to our hearts, *"Here I Am."*

The *"I Am"* of Isaiah is the same *"I Am"* of Exodus introduced to us previously when Moses tells how he asked God to identify himself other than *"The God of your ancestors..."* When Moses was planning his trip to Egypt to lead the Hebrews out of slavery, he was certain they would demand more credentialing than his assurance that he came on behalf of the God who did things in the past. He wanted a powerful name. Instead, God gave him the first person, singular, present indicative of "Be". Moses needed to understand that the Hebrews could not know God other than in terms of their participation in the divine offer of deliverance. In Luke's Gospel, the issue of personal identity surfaced during a dispute among Jesus' followers as to *"which one was to be regarded as the greatest."* Jesus taught them that titles and glorified designations belonged to people with power who exercise earthly authority and refer to themselves as benefactors. He expected His followers to know Him as One who serves.

51

God provides no name that can be dropped as special knowledge. What we can realistically say is limited to repeating what others tell of their joint ventures with God and what we can tell of ours. Who is God? The One among us who inspires, empowers and enlightens us to be **"one who serves."**

> In haunts of wretchedness and need,
> In shadowed thresholds dark with fears,
> From paths where hide the lures of greed,
> We catch the vision of Thy tears.
> —*Frank Mason North*

The Outcome
I Peter 1:1-9

There is no test more challenging than one involving faith in the justice and righteousness of God. In contrast, testing in the natural order provides conceptual and achievable options where material things can be analyzed and productively manipulated with time, patience, intellect, and wisdom. The test of faith calls upon believers to base their response upon objectively unverifiable results. There is no God in a bottle awaiting analysis. Peter indicates that believers must approach testing with the conviction that *"you are receiving a changed life"* that looks to eternity for validation. Whereas nature's tests and results can be measured and defined, the results of faith rest upon God's righteousness and justice, implicated in *"a changed life"* that anticipates fulfillment. Christians value resurrection as the continuation without hindrance of eternal values revealed by Jesus on earth and promoted by His followers after His crucifixion and resurrection. The words of the prophet Micah define validation for people of faith:

"He has told you, O mortal, what is good; and what does the Lord require of you but to do justice, and to love kindness, and to walk humbly with your God." —Micah 6:8

BEHAVIOR IS THE LANGUAGE OF FAITH!

Righteous And Unrighteous
I Peter 3:18-22

Empathy is defined as "the act of entering into the feeling and spirit of others." Undeserved death by crucifixion was Jesus' act of entering into the feeling and spirit of undeserving people in order for us to know God. Such an act draws attention because of the universality of its declaration. The Apostle Paul points out in his letter to the fledging Christian community in Rome that *"rarely would anyone die for a righteous person though perhaps for a good person someone might actually dare to die. But God proves His love for us in that while we were yet sinners Christ died for us."*

The undeserved death of an individual for the benefit of those for whom he feels affection is not rare. Nor is it rare for people to die for a cause in which they strongly believe. The unique attraction of the Christian message is that Jesus of Nazareth is uniquely the Son of God Who unjustly suffered and died to reveal God's empathy for a permanently flawed humanity. Jesus experienced the pain of all for whom He seeks redemption.

To those who have intellectual problems with belief in God and the Biblical accounts of God's involvement in human history, it is more important to understand the message than it

53

is to sneer at the delivery system. If not Jesus, then some other earthly medium would be needed to propagate the belief that there is a Creator who desires the best for creation (that was declared good) and is willing to do what is necessary (within the structure), to free it from bondage to destructive impulses, damaging deeds, and debilitating guilt.

It is important for people to feel forgiven for their destructive thoughts and actions in order to release time and motive to creative living. Who is better qualified to relieve guilt than the One who created all things and became fully human in order to walk the walk, to talk the talk, to die an undeserved death, and to be raised victoriously from the dead? The presence of the risen Lord influences human life and empowers *"good conscience,"* empathy, and the desire to *"love one's neighbor as one's self."*

Amazingly, the message and the associated power have positive results. This is in spite of institutional Christianity that harbors charlatans who implant seeds of exacerbated guilt in order to market a remedy.

It might be comforting for most of us to know that the majority of prominent Biblical characters from Genesis to Revelation were, like us, flawed in character and performance. Yet, God found something to salvage and He influenced them for His purpose. If the time comes that you have the need, take comfort, *"If God"* (who empathizes) *"is for you, who can be against you?"* It is not a bad protocol for those who experience the symptoms and acknowledge the illness.

We by His spirit prove
And know the things of God,
The things which freely of His love
He hath on us bestowed.
—*Charles Wesley*

BEHAVIOR IS THE LANGUAGE OF FAITH!

Discernment And Application
Romans 12:1-21

Conforming to one's surroundings is common sense. It is one of the ways that we avoid pain and experience pleasure. A lot of thoughts and feelings struggle to settle us into the most user-friendly setting. So, what's new?

Paul tells the Christian community in Rome not to conform to the ways of non-Christians that they lived among. He said they needed to be transformed by renewing their minds in order to live a life that conforms to the will of God. He said the Christian life is marked by humility, sober judgment, peace, kindness, and life that is free of revenge. Paul is describing a lifestyle that emphasizes harmony and the Christian's life-long effort to **"overcome evil with good."**

Nine boys, ages twelve to fifteen, gathered their baseball equipment and started walking home from the park where they had been playing since school was over at three o'clock. They hadn't been home since morning when they left for school. They were tired and hungry. It was dusk dark as they walked along the wooden fence surrounding Dr. Hick's backyard. Bryan was the oldest of the group—very popular at school—also best known for getting himself and others into mischief. Saying "no" to him was not easy.

Rather unexpectedly, Bryan shouted, "Stop! I've got a great idea. Let's climb over Dr. Hick's fence and get some apples from his orchard." The other boys didn't seem enthusiastic. "Come on," Bryan said. "With all those trees he wouldn't miss any apples. We haven't eaten since lunch. Come on! Don't be wimps."

Gradually the boys came around to Bryan's persistent pleading. That is, everyone but Russell, who was the smallest. When Bryan told him to step up for a boost, Russell shook his head and said he didn't want to do it.

Bryan insisted "After all, we all agreed to do it."

Russell shook his head no. The other guys joined Bryan in making fun of Russell and putting him down.

Bryan asked, "Why don't you stick with the rest of us like we planned?"

Russell said, "Because my father wouldn't want me to."

Bryan quickly replied, "You mean to tell us that your father specifically told you not to go over Dr. Hick's fence and get some apples?"

Russell said, "No, he has never said anything about Dr. Hick's apples."

Bryan reasoned, "Then how do you know your father gives a damn."

Without hesitation Russell said, "Because I know my father!"

The mind must discern what is good *"without claiming to be wiser than you are."* Paul thought it very important to remind believers to be faithful to God's abiding presence. The timeless value of this lesson comes to us in our awareness of the seemingly innocent temptations that undercut our faith.

> To serve the present age,
> My calling to fulfill;
> May it all my powers engage
> To do my Master's will.
> —*Charles Wesley*

BEHAVIOR IS THE LANGUAGE OF FAITH!

Seen And Unseen
I Samuel 16:1-13

The clear message in this narrative is a reaffirmation that God's evaluation criteria differs from ours. We are limited to outward appearances. He looks at the inner person. So how can we evaluate another person effectively? This is especially important if they are in a position of leadership as was the case with David in I Samuel. Performance is one familiar standard of measure even though everyone, like David, experiences high and low periods of implementation. People recognize and rely upon meritorious performance when they see it over time, even if they are unable to precisely standardize it. Performance will always be the murky window through which we view the inner being of another that is seen clearly by God.

Jesus taught that the legitimate criteria by which we measure our spiritual maturity are the words and deeds by which we live. "You know the tree by the fruit it bears." This is not to be confused with the notion that we are able to earn God's acceptance and praise based upon adherence to laws and codes of conduct that are both tutorial and analytical—tutorial in that they modify behavior *("...without understanding, temper must be curbed with bit and bridle else it will not stay near you"* **Psalm 32:9)**; analytic in that they shed light on severity. This approach is never successful because misapplication encourages self-righteousness and such deception intensifies guilt. Jesus raises the bar to performance-based gratification. Appreciation is the response when one accepts the gift from God that meets one's need. It is interesting to consider that the science of brain imaging might one day be capable of tracking physical changes in the brain that result from experiencing God's forgiveness and our feeling of gratitude.

Then turning toward the woman, He said to Simon, *"Do you see this woman? I entered your house; you gave me no water for my feet, but she has bathed my feet with her tears and dried them with her hair. You gave me no kiss, but from the time I came in she has not stopped kissing my feet. You did not anoint my head with oil, but she has anointed my feet with ointment. Therefore, I tell you, her sins, which are many, have been forgiven; hence, she has shown great love. But the one to whom little is forgiven, loves little."* Luke 7:44-48

Those who do not love feel superior to everyone else.
Those who love feel equal to everyone else.
Those who love much gladly take the lower place.
—*Carlo Carretto*

BEHAVIOR IS THE LANGUAGE OF FAITH!

Resurrection/Release/Subjection
I Corinthians 15:1-28

The GOOD NEWS when received becomes the basis for taking a stand and remaining firm. Paul said the message he received and passed on was that Jesus died for the sins of those who feel the burden and oppression of guilt and need relief. The implication is that there are those who, regardless of the reason, feel no need and have no interest in relief. God's involvement in the relief process is the resurrection of Jesus from the dead. By this, he confirmed the eternal quality of Jesus' life. If anyone has a better way to address the human condition, it's time to step up!

Paul attributed his changed life to the grace of God. He was a persecutor (an understatement) of Christians. Yet, he became a child of grace and worked harder than most in bringing good news to the fields of sin, guilt, and death. In contrast to Paul's new life, his former life was that of a thoroughgoing "institutional man." He employed the *"powers of this world"* to exploit the sinful human condition and appeal to the deepest need for meaning to life. Power, control, and conformity were the most attractive and realistic options. Paul said these options, from which he was transformed, will remain enticingly available until all of their earthly advocates are defeated. WOW!! No place for the faint-hearted; decision time. Guilt is no longer a stumbling block because the path has been cleared and resurfaced with stepping stones. Now, where is our heart? What is our desire?

Sing with all the sons of glory,
Sing the resurrection song!
Death and sorrow, earth's dark story,
To the former days belong.
All around the clouds are breaking,
Soon the storms of time shall cease;
In God's likeness, man awaking,
Knows the everlasting peace.
—*William J. Irons*

Deliverance
Isaiah 25:1-9

Like the prophet, there are many who believe in God and have an opinion about his plan for creation. We experience and observe enough creative and wonderful things in life that we expect more and better things to be in store. Also like the prophet, we experience and observe some degree of suffering and destruction that doesn't make sense. Isaiah is comfortable accepting that God put in place a natural order that is temporary. The system provides for both accomplishment and demolition without detailed clarification. The prophet simply accepts that God alone is eternal and his glorification is the only basis for any lasting human purpose and performance. Eternity must be spoken of through the limitations of myths and

59

metaphors about pearly gates, golden streets, choirs of angels, and God seated upon a throne.

In the creation story, the disobedience of Adam and Eve made them knowledgeable of good and evil. As a result God barred them from the tree of eternal life. The parameters of human life are fixed; *"You are dust and to dust you shall return."* Our earthly effort is directed appropriately when we choose to be tutored by the system created to *"incline our hearts"* toward eternal values.

O Lord, You are my God:
I will exalt You, I will praise Your name;
For You have done wonderful things,
Plans formed of old, faithful and sure.
—Isaiah 25:1

BEHAVIOR IS THE LANGUAGE OF FAITH!

Suffering
I Peter 2:18-25

For someone to desire suffering suggests an emotional disorder. Suffering for a purpose more laudable than personal gratification is an admirable commitment that exists among the non-religious as well as the religious. So what is so appealing about the Apostle Peter's instructions that the endurance of undeserved suffering meets with God's approval?

Slavery was an accepted practice in Peter's day, and he did not challenge the system. Rather, he suggested that the way to effect change is to endure the suffering that an unjust system imposes. People of faith live in hope authenticated by the resurrection of Jesus. The contrast with common practice will provide an opportunity to witness to God's redeeming love that

Jesus embodied. His suffering is the vehicle of our healed relationship with the *"guardian of our souls."*

This passivity is better understood when considered in light of the belief among Peter's contemporaries that the end of time and the return of Jesus were imminent. Social restructuring, in this context, would have been a poor use of time and resources. In the short term, Christians were to accept their earthly station and condition while concentrating upon the message of God's redemption.

Jesus' moral and ethical teachings have much greater appeal to most of us than his sayings that we must be aggressive and *"take up our cross and follow him;"* or, *"are you able to drink from the cup that I drink;"* or, *"the servant is not greater than the master;"* or, Peter's echo, *"Christ also suffered for you, leaving you an example, so that you should follow in his footsteps."* Suffering is no virtue. However, suffering is worthy of notice when it results from faithful devotion to **"Thy will be done on earth as it is in heaven."** We need to disregard attempts to avoid it.

> "The consecrated cross I'll bear
> Till death shall set me free;
> And then go home my crown to wear,
> For there's a crown for me."
> —*Thomas Shepherd*

Nullification
Galatians 2:11-21

When General George Patton refused to retreat in the face of a strong German counterattack, he told his subordinates, "I don't want to pay for the same real estate twice." Paul expressed this same attitude when he confronted Peter and Barnabas on the occasion of their retreat from the fellowship of grace and unity with Gentile Christians because Jewish Christians arrived who continued to combine Jewish legalism with faith in Jesus as Messiah.

Paul viewed the ground gained through the resurrection of Jesus as a unifying presence in the lives of those who accepted his influence. Any evaluation criteria that held to former legalistic loyalties as necessary sidebars to supplement the gospel were considered regressive. He called this hypocrisy and a *"nullification of God's grace."*

Too often, like Peter and Barnabas, we allow the presence of influential people to cause us to modify and retreat from what the risen Lord defeated and secured within our hearts. We must work and pray that in our daily activities he doesn't continue to pay for the same ground twice.

> "After my return home, I was much buffeted with temptations; but cried out, and they fled away. They returned again and again. I as often lifted up my eyes, and He 'sent me help from his holy place.' And herein, I found the difference between this and my former state chiefly consisted. I was striving, yea, fighting with all my might under the law, as well as under grace. But then I was sometimes, if not often, conquered; now, I was always conqueror."
> —*John Wesley*

BEHAVIOR IS THE LANGUAGE OF FAITH!

Recompense
II Corinthians 5:1-10

Earthly life that is pleasing to the Creator is presented Biblically as a brief, but important, prelude to eternity. Some people fortunately enter the world like protected greenhouse seeds planted in biodegradable trays that later are placed in a well-cultivated and fertilized field where the roots are free to reach out and nourish the fruit-bearing plant. Others are not so fortunate and are born into misery. Regardless of circumstances, the plan is for every plant to bear fruit according to the environment. Each plant is evaluated in light of the growing conditions. Every fruit-bearing plant is valued for desirable qualities that might be used to improve other plants. Plants that bear no fruit have no purpose other than to demonstrate what does not need to perpetuate.

> "As men of old their first fruits brought
> Of orchard, flock and field
> To God, the giver of all good,
> The source of bounteous yield;
> So we today first fruits would bring,
> The wealth of this good land,
> Of farm and market, shop and home,
> Of mind and heart and hand."
> —*Frank Von Christierson*

BEHAVIOR IS THE LANGUAGE OF FAITH!

Flesh And Spirit
Galatians 5:13-26

The Biblical creation account tells us that Adam and Eve, after their act of disobedience, hid from God. When God came for His visit in the garden and couldn't find them, He called for them to come out of hiding. He wanted Adam and Eve to exercise the freedom to manage their new-found knowledge of good and evil even though they were overwhelmed by the results of their bad decision. He clothed them and sent

63

them on their way with the hope that they would be mindful of His presence and desire His influence.

The call comes to us as it did to them—the call to creative freedom influenced by divine presence that enhances our ability to manage desires to honor God and serve the common good. The Tester also sends out a call to serve the earthly desires of the flesh. Both calls offer a promotional reward.

Paul lists the desires of the flesh, which focus upon sexual gratification, loyalty to manufactured Gods, antipathy in personal relations, and destructive personal habits. In contrast, the fruit of the Spirit shapes one's disposition, resulting in self-control that overcomes conceit and competition among personalities. It is worth noting that works of the flesh can be itemized. On the other hand, the fruit of the Spirit is entirely dispositional, situational, and outgoing.

"O Lord, my heart is not lifted up,
My eyes are not raised too high;
I do not occupy myself with things
Too great and marvelous for me.
But I have calmed and quieted my soul,
Like a weaned child with its mother;
My soul is like the weaned child that is within me.
O Israel, hope in the LORD
From this time on and forevermore."
—Psalm 131

Weal And Woe
Isaiah 45:1-5

How pleasant it would be if everyone had only wonderful and pleasant things occur in their lives. We know this is fantasy. The natural order allows for random experiences of joy and pain without discernible equity. Neither the godly nor the ungodly have resolved this mystery with anything more than a shrug. Nor, will we. The harsh environment of natural selection appears to be the basic operational system that binds creation. Religion derives from the Latin root *religio;* "to rebind." The Christian religion teaches that Jesus revealed an enhancement to the natural operational system that reflects values, meaning, and purpose that preceded creation and will continue after the natural order ends.

We manage the best we can with the Biblical teaching that *"all things work to the glory of God."* Joy evokes thanksgiving; pain induces cries for relief. Knowledge and understanding are for the adult within us to manage amid this *"weal and woe."* Given that we are forever the child, it appears that our primitive sense of divine presence is reserved by God for the simple, spontaneous, trusting child within us. *"Truly I tell you, whoever does not receive the kingdom of God as a little child will never enter it."*

"O God, our help in ages past,
Our hope for years to come,
Our shelter from the stormy blast,
And our eternal home!"
—*Isaac Watts*

BEHAVIOR IS THE LANGUAGE OF FAITH!

He Gives All
Acts 17:22-32

Christian conviction begins with God *"who gives all..."* With that confirmed in our hearts, we are purged of arrogant effort to form an image with art or language that attempts to define God. Humanity is limited to giving humble expression through personal and communal effort to the miniscule or magnanimous effect of God on life.

Humanity's predisposition toward personal gratification and arrogance before God is captured in this personal recollection, and participation in the life and legends of Columbus County, North Carolina hunting stories—one of which recalls an old Rocky Mountain Coon hound owned by Lacy Gore. His name was Crocket. Few could equal his ability to track and tree a coon in the swamps of southeastern North Carolina.

Crocket had an unusual disposition for a coon hound. He was an incorrigible individualist—not a good thing for his breed because they were bred to run with a pack. The thrill of the hunt was for the hunters to know which dog was first to pick up the coon's track; next priority was to be familiar with each dog's yowl so the hunters could determine which one was leading the pack.

Crocket was fine with these arrangements as long as the other dogs didn't happen to bump him or growl at him during the hunt or when the coon finally went up the tree. The other dogs in the pack expected no such indulgence. When Crocket was offended, he would leave the hunt and go back to the truck and load-up in the dog box—he was through. He refused to participate in any further hunts that night. All of the hunters were familiar with his arrogance. When they gathered up the dogs to go from one place to another and couldn't find Crocket, they assumed he was in the truck sulking. Lacy put up with Crocket's inconvenient ways until he finally came to the conclusion that nothing would change and sold him. It was unfortunate that such breeding, talent, and training was wasted because of canine arrogance—Lacy didn't need to endure it.

God doesn't need human intervention on His behalf. As Paul writes, *"nor is he served by human hands as though he needed anything."* The art form through which God reveals Himself is the effect He has upon transformed desires that reflect His artistry through the behavior of the community of faith.

God does not need us to establish or defend His position. The word need is earthbound. Created things have need. God has no need. The word God, and all words related to divinity, reflect humanity's need that is similar to a child's need for parental presence. Without God, we are spiritual orphans in a universe of tenuous things. Jesus teaches that we should call the Creator *"Father (Life Giver)."* That's comforting!

Immortal, invisible, God only wise,
In light inaccessible hid from our eyes,
Most blessed, most glorious, the Ancient of Days,
Almighty, victorious, Thy great name we praise.
—*Walter Chalmers Smith*

BEHAVIOR IS THE LANGUAGE OF FAITH!

Sacred Presence
Isaiah 63:7-9

The Prophet Isaiah reminds the *"people of God"* how the *"gracious deeds"* of God were poured out to their benefit. They were undeserved deeds of mercy, not rewards for devoted service. Unfortunately, the recipients did not respond with grateful appreciation.

The plan of God was to reveal His righteous, just, and forgiving presence to the world through obvious expressions of appreciation by an undeserving insignificant people who had no other asset but God to account for their good fortune. The Prophet reminded them that they were looked upon by their contemporaries as *"the least of all nations,"* that their father Abraham was a *"wondering Aramean,"* and that they served as slaves in Egypt until God's deliverance. Nothing in their natural history suggests being a "cut above."

Contrary to God's wishes, the *"blessed chosen"* viewed themselves as the "chosen blessed." Rather than *"blessed"*

67

people chosen to witness, they viewed themselves as **chosen** people whose blessings were evidence of qualitative difference. The reorder of two words resulted in elevating the recipient rather than the benefactor. God took *"no people"* and made them *"His people."* Who did Isaiah say was the gift giver? *"No messenger or angel, but His presence saved them."* The continuation of redemption methodology is recognized in Isaiah's description of God's suffering servant.

> *"Who has believed our message and to whom has the arm of the Lord been revealed? He grew up before Him like a tender shoot, And like a root out of dry ground. He had no beauty or majesty to attract us to him, nothing in his appearance that we should desire him. He was despised and rejected by men, a man of sorrows and acquainted with suffering. Like one from whom men hide their faces, He was despised, and we esteemed Him not. Surely He took up our infirmities and carried our sorrows, yet we considered Him stricken by God, smitten by Him, and afflicted. But He was pierced for our transgressions; He was crushed for our iniquities; the punishment that brought us peace was upon Him, and by His wounds we are healed. We all, like sheep, have gone astray; each of us has turned to his own way, and the LORD has laid on him the iniquity of us all." —Isaiah 53:1-6*

BEHAVIOR IS THE LANGUAGE OF FAITH!

Truth In Love
Ephesians 4:1-16

D o you recall having to write a 300-word theme in High School English class? It didn't sound like much, but before it was completed you were counting words and searching for just the right filler that reached the number while maintaining the integrity of the theme. *"Truth In Love"* is the three-word theme of Christian faith that is not diminished by its brevity.

Whatever we say and do should be conditioned by *"truth in love."* Paul lists characteristics of the *"worthy life as humility, gentleness, patience, bearing with one another in love, unity, peace, one body, one spirit, one hope, one Lord, one faith, and one baptism."*

These characteristics remain on track only when they are united by *"truth in love."* Truth is the subjective mechanism by which we put facts and feelings together. When numerous people have positive results, it is worth thoughtful consideration.

More often than not, truth presented as a sign of superiority is resisted rather than assimilated. Negative responses are modified when one-upmanship, threats, condemnation, and jealously are removed. *"Truth in love"* unifies a variety of worthy activities in a way that God is glorified and His purpose served.

Thou art the Way, the Truth, the Life;
Grant us that way to know,
That truth to keep, that life to win,
Whose joys eternal flow.
—*George W. Doane*

BEHAVIOR IS THE LANGUAGE OF FAITH!

Things In Common
Acts 2:43-47

Communal living is a hybrid arrangement that might appeal to the imagination of some, but implementation is usually short-lived. First century Christians attempted it in the name of Christ as a way to implement his focus upon physical and spiritual needs that resulted from conditions that were beyond the control of the needy. There were health issues, impoverished widows and orphans, blind beggars, and those oppressed by spiritual guilt.

Christian communal living was frequently an unsuccessful effort based upon the anticipated early return of Jesus who was to preside over the end of time. When this did not materialize, the communal arrangement became unsustainable. Too few participants wanted to produce life's necessities for the benefit of too many that limited their efforts to praying and eating.

Although their timing was off regarding the end of time, their concern for sharing life's necessities was an important expression of spiritual development. *"Generous hearts"* and *"praising God"* are basic to Christian witness. The material world is necessarily an important temporary concern. However, both scientist and prophet tell us that this earthly life will end, leaving a cinder floating about in the cosmos. The permanent issue for Christians is balance between necessity and generosity regardless of the social structure.

> We bear the strain of earthly care,
> But bear it not alone;
> Beside us walks our brother Christ
> And makes our task his own.
> Through din of market, whirl of wheels,
> And thrust of driving trade,
> We follow where the Master leads,
> Serene and unafraid.
> —Ozora S.Davis

Holy Life
Romans 12:1-21

For most people, growing in holiness requires a different way of thinking and different criteria for evaluating good. We have to dismantle and restructure in order to produce different results. It's much more exasperating than learning to brush your teeth with your secondary rather than dominant hand. Can we ever become comfortable and rid ourselves of the remnants of what has been? Thanks be to God from Whom we receive the motivation and power to develop an improved structure that shapes performance.

A pivotal characteristic in developing a holy life is *"not to think of one's self too highly"* because holiness results from a reliance upon God's sacred presence as the dominant influence. The Bible paints a picture of good and evil, the most powerful forces in the universe, engaged in an ongoing battle for control. We are left to choose under which power we wish to live. Both good and evil offer an attractive reward program. Evaluation is measured by how well the individual's role reflects upon the lifestyle promoted by the one chosen as the dominant influence. Christians must be mindful that we are witness to, and reliant upon, the transforming power of God to *"overcome evil with good."*

> Assert Thy claim, receive Thy right,
> Come quickly from above,
> And sink me to perfection's height,
> The depth of humble love.
> —*Charles Wesley*

BEHAVIOR IS THE LANGUAGE OF FAITH!

When You Heard
Ephesians 1:3-14

When my uncle John died, as administrator of his estate, I set a time and place for our widely-scattered family to gather at his Florida home for disposition of his possessions. He owned all of the family heirlooms. Only a few family members came. Most of the other relatives promptly responded, "There is nothing there that I want."

The Bible teaches that God sent messengers, and then Jesus, to proclaim to their contemporaries the inheritance planned by God from the beginning. The call itemized what was available, but few responded with interest because there was nothing they wanted.

I am reminded of what Santa Clause brought Sam Gore when he was fourteen years old. Christmas morning he and his three siblings rushed into the living room to see what had been placed by the fireplace during the night. One of Sam's gifts was in a long narrow box wrapped in green Christmas paper decorated with pictures of big buck deer. Sam was certain the box contained a new gun. With paper off and the end of the box opened, he turned the box upside down and out slipped a beautiful new top-of-the-line ax for chopping firewood. Sam's daddy, Mr. S.P. was grinning from ear to ear. Then it dawned on Sam. When it was his time to cut firewood, he would habitually delay as long as he could and complain that his ax was so old and chipped that he couldn't put an edge on it—he needed a new ax.

Never in his wildest imagination did he intend for that to be understood as a Christmas request. Happily, Sam received other gifts that he appreciated much more. However, complaining about cutting firewood was over. Justifying inactivity because of what we don't have might result in receiving what we need to do what God wants done.

God customizes the same inheritance notification for every generation. The important question remains "Is there anything that anyone wants?" Those who humbly receive their inheritance are pleased to honor their benefactor by putting it to good use. Those who want nothing receive nothing. They remain delightfully busy with other interests.

> Though there be dark, uncharted space,
> With worlds on worlds beyond our sight,
> Still may we trust Thy love and grace,
> And wait Thy word, Let Thee be light.
> —*Elizabeth Burrowes*

BEHAVIOR IS THE LANGUAGE OF FAITH!

Nearsighted
II Peter 1:1-12

Faith in God's forgiveness and sharing his divine nature is sustained through cultivating goodness, knowledge, self-control, endurance, godliness, mutual affection, and love. These qualities enhance effective witness to God's presence and purpose in serving the common good. Absent these qualities, personal desire clouds one's inner vision, resulting in spiritual nearsightedness.

God's work is near and far. We must look inward and outward in order to be effective. Spiritual nearsightedness is the primary mechanism by which evil neutralizes the effect of God's grace. When we succumb to the temptation to focus upon things near, the gift of God's redemption is ensconced in the bubble of personal religion that fails to recognize and serve the common good.

Goodness, knowledge, self-control, and endurance are desirable personal attributes that add to the quality of a well-managed life and provide valuable near vision. However, distant vision that affects those beyond ourselves involves godliness,

73

mutual affection, and love. These three imbue us with an interest in the common good, without which, faith is least effective and, at worst, counterproductive by projecting a self-righteous image.

O Thou Who dost the vision send
And givest each his task,
And with the task sufficient strength:
Show us Thy will, we ask.
Give us a conscience bold and good;
Give us a purpose true,
That it may be our highest joy,
Our Fathers work to do.
            —*Jay T. Stocking*

BEHAVIOR IS THE LANGUAGE OF FAITH!

Protective Relationship
John 17:1-19

In the Lord's Prayer we pray, *"...Lead us not into temptation, but deliver us from evil."* Jesus taught us to ask for God's protection from the power of the Tempter. In our meditation scripture, Jesus again prays to God for the protection of those who believe in Him as the one who discloses life as it was intended to be lived from the beginning.

Christians *"do not belong to this world, therefore, they are hated."* This conflict of purpose and values cannot be reconciled. Christians accept the life, death, and resurrection of Jesus as an example of how a meaningful relationship with the

Creator affects the life He created. This lifestyle conflicts with those responding only to secular priorities.

Creation has a built-in quality control mechanism which the Bible refers to as the Tempter, Satan, the Devil, Beelzebub, etc. (a name for the occasion). The Evil One fulfilled his job description from the beginning with Adam and Eve, then really showed off for God in the handling of Job. He was ineffective when confronting Jesus, who remained constant in his relationship with God and on track with sacred purpose. The Apostle Paul described the faithfulness of Jesus: *"He emptied himself, taking the form of a slave, being born in human likeness. And being in human form, he humbled himself and became obedient to the point of death—even death on a cross. Therefore, God also highly exalted him and gave him the name that is above every name,"* (Philippians 2:7-9)

We clearly recognize why Jesus taught us that a protective relationship with God is necessary in an environment with a difficult built-in testing arrangement. God, through Jesus, encourages his children to remain close for protection, without which, in a state of unacknowledged weakness, we succumb to the Tempter who is too powerful and practiced for us to defeat alone.

Commonality
Acts 4:32-37

Egalitarian social and economic structures are not Christian goals. However, first century Christians had no interest in social structures because the imminent return of Jesus would make them irrelevant. The Book of Acts reported a failed attempt at common ownership of possessions, avoidance of marriage and bearing children, and the cessation of work. However, the first generation of Christian converts turned out not to be the last generation. Therefore, communal living subsided.

Fortunately, compassion for people with spiritual and physical needs replaced communal living as a priority. Over the centuries this has proven to be a significant challenge to the Christian community. We are called upon to be practical as we live *"in the world"* but adopt primary values that are *"not of the world."* This is not dualistic. Rather, it is a matter of prioritizing and managing. We are reminded by Harry Emerson Fosdick that this arrangement requires that we think, work, and pray. We have the promise of Jesus that we would not be left to do this alone. He will **"be with us always"** to *"incline our hearts"* and empower the love of God and neighbor.

"When we walk with the Lord In the light of his word,
What a glory he sheds on our way!
While we do his good will,
He abides with us still,
And with all who will trust and obey."
—*John H. Simmis*

BEHAVIOR IS THE LANGUAGE OF FAITH!

Awaken And Receive

Zechariah 4:1-10

An angel roused the Prophet from a condition compared to being asleep. What resulted from his awakening is the realization that significant creative accomplishments result from the Creator's involvement, not from the sole power and might of human effort. Typically, the human exercise of power is for personal advantage and it generates resistance of like kind and superior effort.

God's creative presence is *recognized* because it redeems and restores. God is not represented in the Bible as threatened by anything done in heaven or on earth. Therefore, divine exercise of might and power would serve no purpose when responding to human visions of grandeur. The Creator perpetuates the creative process by offering options that reflect divine purpose through the exercise of justice and righteousness.

Jesus taught that *"God alone is good."* Therefore, all good things on earth are derivative. The good that we do results when we align our will with God's will. We are taught to pray, *"Thy will be done on earth as it is in heaven."* Our prayer acknowledges the need for our desires to become the same as God's desires. When this occurs, we, like Zechariah, are awakened, receive the Spirit, and become the hands that serve.

What though the world deceitful prove,
And earthly friends and hopes remove;
With patient uncomplaining love,
Still would I cling to Thee.
—*Charlotte Elliott*

Ignorance And A Hard Heart
Ephesians 4:17-5:2

What a simple diagnosis: *"ignorance"* and *"a hard heart."* Similar to a physical illness, all that's needed is a simple one or two-word description that can mean a lifetime of treatment and rehabilitation. Members of the Christian community in Ephesus had **"lost all sensitivity,"** and were exhibiting behavior that was no different from people who were insensitive to God's influence. Greed and unmanaged sexual activity were evidence that nothing had changed in their lives. Paul asked them to reflect upon the teachings and activities of Jesus because he was the embodiment of the truth and the righteousness of God.

Holiness in thought and deed are the twin towers of God's grace. His presence inspires more than a revised word track. It inspires and empowers creative change in thoughts, feelings, and habits. God does not fancy sharing space with evil. Therefore, when God's presence influences desire, there is no compromised space shared with evil.

We participate in a life-long eviction process, during which the comforts and conveniences of evil are programmed for displacement. Jesus emphasized this in the parable of the Evicted Demons who conveniently moved back in the unoccupied human life because after their eviction they were not replaced with the transforming presence of God. Paul sets the bar high when he writes, Wisdom and zeal and faith impart, **"be imitators of God...live in love as Christ loved us ...a fragrant offering..."**

Firmness with meekness from above,
To bear thy people on their heart,
And love the souls whom thou dost love.
—*James Montgomery*

Heirs By Adoption
Romans 8:1-17

One thing about which theologians and scientists generally agree is that life on earth had a beginning and it will end. Christians consider life to be a gift from God, while also believing that the Creator encoded a sunset factor. The creation story in Genesis makes it clear that the gift of life forever remains under the Creator's total control. To drive home the point we are provided the image of an angel with a flaming sword guarding the *"tree of life"* to prevent humanity, with its newly acquired knowledge, from achieving perpetuity.

Amid this life and death cycle is sensitivity to an eternal dimension that one might describe as spiritual awareness. Whether life beyond death is collective wishful thinking, or a built-in sensitivity that operates like a compass, no one knows for a fact. Regardless, spiritual awareness, as well as knowledge, is an important part of the human motivational system. For those who are willing to respond to Divine presence, there is the gift of the Spirit that dynamically bonds the recipient, as an adopted child, to the Creator, who is known through the just and righteous life of Jesus.

I thank thee, Lord, that thou hast kept the best in store;
We have enough, yet not too much, to long for more;
A yearning for a deeper peace not known before.
—*Adelaide A. Procter*

BEHAVIOR IS THE LANGUAGE OF FAITH!

Inherit
Matthew 25:31-46

Property boundaries are sited by identifying a known starting point and following the coordinates described on the deed. Modern land surveyors find it difficult to follow instructions on an old deed that gives a description such as, "go to a point beginning at the big oak tree at the corner of the old Jones field"; or, "Begin at a point in the bend of the road before Smith's Creek Bridge." Property boundaries are established today with satellite coordinates related to Geodetic Survey markers set in cement. The life and teachings of Jesus defined the coordinates permanently established by God for those who will inherit the kingdom prepared from the beginning. The landscape constantly changes, but the boundary lines remain in place.

God's kingdom is an inheritance, not something earned or deserved. God alone knows for certain which of his children have an interest in the same things that interest him. Jesus indicates that God is not going to burden anyone with an inheritance that generates no interest. I am reminded of a very dear friend who has for many years owned and tended a farm. He was concerned about how he would divide it among his three children. He asked each one of them about their interest in the farm. Two of them expressed an interest in owning the farm no longer than it would take to sell it. The third wanted it with the hope that a grandson would also have an interest when the time came. Who do you think inherited the farm? Who do you think will inherit the kingdom Jesus revealed?

> I'll praise my Maker while I have breath;
> And when my voice is lost in death,
> Praise shall employ my nobler powers.
> My days of praise shall ne'er be past,
> While life, and thought, and being last,
> Or immortality endures.
> —Isaac Watts

Great And First
Matthew 20:20-29

Theological schizophrenia is being ***in the world, but not of the world.*** Jesus presented a two-world option that requires very different behavior and contrasting reward structures. The world of our conception and birth starts us out with a strong sense of entitlement. We demand to be fed and comforted or else we loudly complain. From birth until death we strive for more superior forms of gratification.

Along the way we are introduced to the needs and desires of others that are equally as intense as ours. We adjust. Next, we are introduced to another dimension of life that involves a presence that is sensed, yet, not defined by the senses. We might or might not take up with this spiritual dimension. If we do, personal awareness becomes collective as we encounter others with a similar experience.

There is a clear contrast between our birth orientation, the immeasurable unseen divine presence, and the demonstrated unselfish servitude to community wellbeing in the life and teachings of Jesus. He lived his life for others.

"With a child's glad heart of love
At thy bidding may I move
Prompt to serve and follow thee,
Loving him who first loved me."
—Jane E. Leeson

BEHAVIOR IS THE LANGUAGE OF FAITH!

Instruct Me
Psalm 16

"**N**o good apart from God,**"** is a basic Biblical truth. Good exists only in relationships. First with God (Jesus said, **"God alone is good"**), and then with others. When we attempt to go it alone by arming ourselves with only knowledge and wisdom, the result is diminished. In contrast, history and modernity provide examples of people with talents, of varying degrees and kinds, who do marvelous things as a result of being *"blessed by the counsel of the Lord... instructing their heart."* Their persistent witness is that *"by keeping the Lord before me...I shall not be moved."*

Doing good, in conjunction with a motivating and enabling power greater than one's self, results in an enhanced level of *"gladness..., rejoicing..., and contentment."* St Augustine prayed, "Thou hast made me for thyself alone, and my soul is restless until it finds its rest in thee." We, therefore, join him and the Psalmist in praying, *"You show me the path of life."*

Give to the wind thy fears;
Hope and be undismayed;
God hears thy sighs, and counts thy tears,
God shall lift up thy head.
—*Paul Gerhardt*, translated by John Wesley

BEHAVIOR IS THE LANGUAGE OF FAITH!

Strive First
Matthew 6:25-34

Physical needs are obviously important, especially if one is deprived. A thirsty, hungry, cold person is passionately concerned with nothing other than addressing these needs. For this reason the Bible questions the value of prosperous people acknowledging the deprivation of others without providing the opportunity for relief. *"If a brother or sister is naked and lacks daily food, and one of you says to them, 'Go in peace; keep warm and eat your fill,' and yet you do not supply their bodily needs, what is the good of that (James 2:15-16)"?*

The physical world makes available the resources for addressing physical needs. Developing and sustaining an adequate distribution system is a perennial challenge because immature human desire aggressively looks inward and has little left for interest in the needs of others.

Jesus teaches that when one *"strives first for the kingdom of God and his righteousness, all these things will be given to you as well."* Awareness of God's presence provides the motivation and the maturity for addressing deprivation. Absent the motivation, we have a diagnosis without a remedy. Prioritizing is important.

"Follow the reverent steps the great example
Of him whose holy work was doing good;
So shall the wide earth seem our Father's temple,
Each loving life a psalm of gratitude."
—*John Greenleaf Whittier*

BEHAVIOR IS THE LANGUAGE OF FAITH!

83

Spirit Led
I Corinthians 2:1-11

Paul makes it clear; uniform purpose is primarily spirit-led activity supported by uniform practice. He makes no effort to evaluate the effectiveness of his personal efforts, nor does he attempt to validate their authenticity. His instructions are clear, **"each is given the manifestation of the Spirit for the common good."**

The common good is too often a less effective motivator than an appeal to personal satisfaction. Many of us have a powerful inclination to imagine ourselves on center stage regardless of the role we play. This is one reason why religious motivators find it more productive to accentuate personal appeal by describing the blessings of the good life or chumming for the redemption of the downcast. However, most effective Christians have qualities similar to a first-class coon-hound; both must function harmoniously.

Crocket was one quality away from being a top-notch coon-hound. He was powerfully built; a nose that could follow a coon on land or water; and too intelligent to be outsmarted by a coon on the run. Lacy was Crocket's owner; a skilled coon hunter and a charter member of the local coon hunter's association. The association sponsored an early fall coon-hound water contest that allowed dogs to compete in a swimming race to see which dog could swim the lake and be first to bark up the tree where a live coon was place out of reach in a wire cage.

Regulations required all competing dogs to be in a kennel placed at the water's edge. They could clearly see the coon in a cage on a small float with a rope attached that allowed it to be pulled across the lake just out of reach of the dogs that were simultaneously released from the kennel to chase the coon. The winning dog was the first one to bark at the coon up the tree. Pride of ownership, and an occasional side bet, was sufficient to guarantee a get-together of coon hunters.

When the starting gun sounded and the kennel doors opened, it was difficult to identify any particular dog because they simultaneously hit the water splashing and barking.

Visibility cleared within a few seconds of the initial splash and the crowd was able to see the progress of each dog. Lacy, along with other Crocket supporters, immediately became concerned because they couldn't pick out Crocket. Hubert shouted to Lacy, "Do you reckon they drowned him?" Lacy didn't believe that for one moment; however, Crocket was not in sight. Sam said, "Lacy, look behind you." There was Crocket; sitting on the lake shore with the hunters; he refused to participate. Lacy wasted his entry fee and lost his wager because Crocket was offended when Lacy put him in a kennel with a pack of strange dogs bumping into him and growling. Crocket was very sensitive and frequently would pout and sulk if he was put in a situation that didn't suit him. The water race was one of those situations. The problem with owning a coon-dog with Crocket's disposition is that coon hunting is primarily done with a pack of dogs working together to tree a coon in the wild where the coon is familiar with the surroundings. There is no place on a coon hunt for a coon-hound with an attitude. Crocket's natural assets and skills were wasted because he wouldn't function harmoniously with other coon-hounds.

"All things work for good for those who love the Lord" because the common good is the work in which the Creator is involved. Christians must be continually mindful of the tension that exists between personal gratification and common good as we daily respond to the guiding presence of the Holy Spirit.

O living church, Thine errand speed;
Fulfill thy task sublime;
With bread of life Earth's hunger feed;
Redeem the evil time.
—*Samuel Longfellow*

My Mind-My Flesh
Romans 7:14-25

Paul's observations regarding inner conflict have not passed with time. Reason might adequately inform us of the options that provide dependable long-term benefit. Yet, we too frequently prefer instant gratification, even when we are aware of the undesirable consequences. Paul's world view prompted him to urgently tell his readers that their bodies, subject to death and decay, are incapable of managing themselves responsibly. No matter how strong-willed we perceive ourselves to be, our bodies consistently orient toward immediate desires and perceived needs.

Only when values reorient, does will, knowledge, and wisdom begin to develop and affirm a purpose more worthy than momentary personal indulgence. Social traditions, governmental structures, scientific method, and religious codes (prostheses for deformed hearts) are evidence of the unrealistic challenge to implement more than temporary modifications. These arrangements are valuable mitigating mechanisms that address the human condition. Within this context, there is a persistent awareness of Sacred Presence that offers to elevate our thoughts and modify our desires as the way to override arrogance in favor of *"doing justice, loving kindness, and walking humbly before God."*

"Take my will, and make it thine;
It shall be no longer mine.
Take my heart; It is thine own;
It shall be thy royal throne.
Take my love; my Lord I pour
At thy feet its treasure store.
Take myself, and I will be ever, only all for thee."
—*Frances R. Havergal*

BEHAVIOR IS THE LANGUAGE OF FAITH!

Stumbling Abounds
Luke 17:1-6

People generally find it difficult to forgive a significant personal offense. For this reason we rejoice when our relationship with God frees us from the perpetual need to lament over our unkind attitudes concerning the actions of others that cannot be changed. However, reviewing the past is very important in maintaining a creative life. A backward and forward perspective prevents us from drifting sideways rather than making progress toward the desired goal. Two reference points are always necessary to maintain a course. The rear view is a reference to where we have been and do not wish to return. The forward view is where we wish to go without digressing.

The disciples were overwhelmed because Jesus told them that repentance, forgiveness, and transformation are never a "done deal" in this life. Occasions for stumbling are bound to occur. We, like the disciples, have limited faith with which to address a myriad of personal issues. We need to mark in our minds and hearts the past hazards so we can avoid them. We want common good to replace personal advantage as the hub of our spiritual space and the clear destination for which we maintain a course. This is the context within which repentance, forgiveness, redemption, and transformation reflects the influential presence and purpose of the power of God by which all things were, and are, created.

"Be still my soul: the Lord is on thy side;
Bear patiently the cross of grief or pain;
Thy hope thy confidence let nothing shake,
All now mysterious shall be bright at last.
Be still my soul: The waves and winds still know
His voice who ruled them while down below."
—*Katharina Von Schlegel*

BEHAVIOR IS THE LANGUAGE OF FAITH!

Two Or More
I Corinthians 2:1-13

Religion is about the challenge of three-party communications when one party is without form. The Bible teaches that where two or more are gathered in God's name, He is there also. Two or more see, speak, and hear each other. The formless presence is an influential awareness that defies definitive articulation but affects how people live. We refer to this presence as God, who neither hypothesizes nor debates. He makes himself known and leaves knowledge, understanding, and wisdom for the *"two or more"* to articulate and implement. Implementation is consistently the more difficult. As a result, time and talent too frequently spend time perfecting form at the expense of content.

The Bible teaches that wisdom predates creation. Words have always been inadequate and do not objectively speak of anything that is not created. Activity is the best evidence of the presence that alone makes known the *"depths of God."*

Holy Spirit, faithful guide,
Hear the Christian's side,
Gently lead us by the hand,
Pilgrims in a desert land;
Weary souls fore'er rejoice,
While they hear the sweetest voice,
Whispering softly, "Wanderer, come!
Follow me, I'll guide thee home."
—*Marcus M. Wells*

BEHAVIOR IS THE LANGUAGE OF FAITH!

Power To Heal
John 5:1-15

Power belongs to God. Those who believe in God accept this. In the beginning, power created order out of chaos. God's power remains in control. The Biblical writers, in a pre-scientific world, viewed the created order as the language that God used to demonstrate his power. They were in awe of divine power when human effort was ineffective during natural disasters. Does the natural order communicate humility in your view?

Jesus plays upon the theme of power over nature when he publicly asked an invalid, ***"Do you want to be made well?"*** For thirty-eight years this man reposed by the healing waters without result. Jesus said to him, ***"stand up..."*** The man walked away healed. Jesus effectively communicated the presence and power of God.

Jesus provided contrast between the language of religious laws and the language of dynamic change. Carefully constructed concepts and inspirational words are important only as accessories to behavior. Behavior is the message. The power of God transforms behavior.

<p align="center">Come thou almighty King,
Help us thy name to sing,
Help us to praise!
Father all glorious,
O'er all victorious,
Come and reign over us,
Ancient of days!
—<i>Anonymous</i></p>

BEHAVIOR IS THE LANGUAGE OF FAITH!

Spiritually Together
Ephesians 2

L ife is a gift of natural desires and senses activated by a mixture of inclinations from a Life Giver who contends with attitudes that de-emphasize commonality. The apostle Paul tells us that the plan of creation is for people to *"be joined together and grow into a holy temple...built spiritually into a dwelling place for God."* The Creator's gift of Jesus provides the cornerstone by which believers develop and align desires, senses, and activities to this end. The modern term "personal salvation" is used as a witness to Christian faith, although it is not a Scriptural term. Biblical writers did not focus upon the word "personal" in relation to faith. They refer to the individual as one *"joined together"* in worship and service to God's will as revealed in Jesus' life. Paul tells the Ephesian church, *"We have access in one Spirit to the Father."* Personal salvation, like personal license plates on a modern vehicle, appeals to desires and senses that motivate some of us to pay extra to have it displayed. In contrast, salvation that *"joins us together"* glorifies God.

Blest be the tie that binds
Our hearts in Christian love:
The fellowship of kindred minds
Is like to that above.
—*John Fawcett*

BEHAVIOR IS THE LANGUAGE OF FAITH!

Newness Of Life
Romans 6:1-14

The purpose of The Laws of Moses is to control passions and their unbridled destruction. Thankfully, God's grace goes beyond legalistic control to effect change. The Bible presents the change as between life and death. Such a dramatic contrast is overwhelming. Paul offered this behavior-modification program to an audience that was primarily legalistic Jews who were oriented toward containment not to reprogramming desires and senses. The Law relieves symptoms and provides a behavioral maintenance code for modifying the effect of a force we name evil that is similar to a debilitating, but not instantly fatal, savage virus. While the Law affects symptoms, God's grace deals directly with human will that is the core of the infection. Prayer and meditation permeate human life with God's will that strengthens desire to be just in human relations and righteous before God. Take heart, the program is customized.

> I sought the Lord, and afterward
> I knew He moved my soul to seek him, seeking me;
> It was not I that found, O Savior true;
> No, I was found of thee.
> —*Anonymous,* The Pilgrim Hymn 1904

BEHAVIOR IS THE LANGUAGE OF FAITH!

Common Joy
II Corinthians 2:3

We know from Paul's other writings that he puts emphasis upon the common good as a basis for evaluating activities done in the name of Jesus. By this, he means common benefit in contrast to faith that centers upon personal spiritual advantage. The Bible verse for today says that common good results in common joy. No consideration is given to personal joy apart from the joy experienced by the community of faith. Too frequently Christians include, or exclude, themselves from activities of the community of believers based on a personal pleasure rating. Paul would have us re-evaluate this criteria for participation.

We often play games with children because of the joy and pleasure it brings the child. The joy of the adult is the joy of the child. A skilled athlete enjoys participating with amateurs, not for personal benefit, but for the sake of the sport that continually needs new well-trained players. Similarly, Christian faith subordinates exclusive personal gratification to communal benefit because in this way we honor the Father about whom Jesus said, **"It is not the will of your Father in heaven that one of these little ones should be lost."** Common joy is vital to Christian nurture. Common good anticipates the participation of both the mature and the maturing.

Thou art giving and forgiving,
Ever blessing ever blest,
Well-spring of the joy of living,
Ocean depth of happy rest!
Thou our Father, Christ our brother,
All who live in love are thine;
Teach us how to love each other,
Lift us to the joy divine.
—Henry Van Dyke

House Of God
Genesis 28:10-17

God *"stood beside"* Jacob, who, in his dream, saw transactions between heaven and earth. God identified himself to Jacob in terms of the effect he had upon Jacob's father and grandfather. God reiterated the blessing and promise he made to them and told Jacob that he too would be blessed and would become a blessing to others. Jacob was initially surprised that God did not confront him in a formal place of worship. However, he came to acknowledge that any place God is present is an *"awesome place,"* a **"house of God,"** a *"gate of heaven."*

In the fullness of time, Jesus expanded upon Jacob's experience when he described the body of believers, individually and collectively, as the holy dwelling place of God whose presence is evidenced by deeds. Actions might prompt an uninitiated observer to ask, "Why did you do that?" In contrast, only words are required to answer questions concerning beliefs. The strength of Christian testimony is "God awareness" that is based upon the effect of His presence. Those who are affected, are credentialed to utilize knowledge and understanding when attempting to speak meaningfully about results.

God only knows the love of God;
O that it now were shed abroad
In this poor stony heart!
For thee I long, for love divine;
This only portion, Lord, be mine;
Be mine this better part!
—*Charles Wesley*

BEHAVIOR IS THE LANGUAGE OF FAITH!

He Has Heard
Psalm 28

The Bible repeatedly tells us about two major categories of people: those who call upon God out of a felt need, and those that **"do not regard the works of the Lord"** because they do not feel the need for deity. Simple enough! Both pathways offer gratifying consequences. Those who call upon God with *"trust in their hearts find strength."* Those who feel no need for God are **"rewarded according to the works of their hands."** Jesus restates the same message by saying that those who disregard God *"have their own reward."*

Satan tempted Jesus by offering a variety of options, each with clearly defined rewards. He is presented in the Bible as the personification of evil, offering elaborate joint ventures with clearly defined rewards. This remains Satan's powerful selling point. His excellent deals offer to pay off quickly and tangibly as in the story of Adam and Eve and the forbidden fruit, the original example of "be careful for what you wish."

In contrast, God offers a covenant relationship in which He unilaterally defines conditions that are optional but not negotiable. God covenants for the common good. (Old Covenant of commandments and New Covenant of grace). His reward system stretches over the long haul. God and Satan each offer an awards program that is consistent with their respective values.

Consecrate me now to thy service Lord,
By the power of grace divine;
Let my soul look up with a steadfast hope,
And my will be lost in thine.
—*Fanny J. Crosby*

Testing Before Blessing
Genesis 32

Jacob was tested by his father-in-law who required him to work fourteen years before permitting marriage to his preferred daughter Rachel. Jacob stayed the course and ended up with two wives and considerable wealth. One could say that Jacob prevailed because he got what he wanted. Jacob was next tested by God during a dream in which he wrestled with an angel from whom he wanted a blessing. Jacob remained in the struggle, even with an injury, until he received the much-desired blessing. He limped for the rest of his life as a result of his injury, but his life was changed for the better to such a degree that his name changed from Jacob to Israel.

Is there any way to miss the point that struggle is a significant factor in spiritual development that benefits the common good? This is consistent with the natural order where enhancements usually, but not always, come as a result of someone's vigorous struggle with adversity. Spiritual development involves a tougher struggle because both our Tester and our Advocate are too powerful for any individual to be an independent player. The will and power to be creative or destructive are derivative; based upon commitment.

Jesus taught us to pray, *"lead us not into temptation (inclinations and influences we cannot manage), but deliver us from evil (a power too great for us alone to defeat)."* To borrow and adapt terms from Mind Games (an article in The New Yorker by John Cassidy) testing, struggling, and blessing might be important stimuli of the prefrontal cortex and the limbic areas of the brain as they affect spiritual planning and development. The former encourages pre-commitment to a reasoned plan of spiritual development as expressed in the "asymmetric paternalism" of religious commandments and codes. The latter favors "hyperbolic spiritual discounting" wherein people treat immediate rewards differently from the way they treat delayed rewards—preferring the former, for inexplicable reasons, when immediate rewards might be self-defeating. This scientific theory, derived from neuroimaging,

95

assumes that the brain has two warring sides. This is a point that theological language has traditionally assumed. At the risk of appearing to be cute, I thought non-Biblical words, although awkward, might be a way to broaden knowledge and understanding.

What peaceful hours I once enjoyed!
How sweet their memory still!
But they have left an aching void
The world can never fill.
—*William Cowper*

BEHAVIOR IS THE LANGUAGE OF FAITH!

Works Of Wisdom
James 3:13-18

"**S**treetwise" is applied to those whose experience makes them aware of the multitudinous situations that might cause harm. The Bible uses the word **"wisdom"** in a similar way to describe someone who is "God conscious." Wisdom from God identifies and warns us that **"bitter envy"** and **"selfish ambition"** are destructive because they are **"earthly, unspiritual, and devilish."** On the creative side of the ledger, God's wisdom lists **"pure, peaceable, gentle, willingness to yield, full of kindness, and good fruits."**

Meditation enables us to quietly consider a broad range of creative possibilities that address the common good and honor the Creator. Contemplation brings specific opportunities to the forefront and creates a mental picture of how we might be personally engaged. Prayer petitions God for the power to act. As a practical matter, **"earthly wisdom"** is developed in response to a natural environment that appeals to self-centeredness in order to survive. In contrast, *"wisdom from above"* searches for harmony through **"common purpose."** Unfortunately, we are not born wise. Wisdom must be received from God and cultivated through a lifetime of meditation, contemplation, prayer, and experience.

"For God's foolishness is wiser than human wisdom, and God's weakness is stronger than human strength."
—I Corinthians 1:25

BEHAVIOR IS THE LANGUAGE OF FAITH!

The Promise
Hebrews 11:1-39

The promises of God constitute the heart of the Biblical message. The Old Covenant was God's promise to Abraham. The New Covenant is Jesus' promise to the community of faith. Both continue to rely upon their respective interpretation of the promise. Jews look for the Messiah. Christians look for the Messiah's return. Paul said, "Yet, all these, though they were commended for their faith, did not receive what was promised."

Doing the right thing is an act of faith because it certainly doesn't consistently produce immediate beneficial results. At the very beginning, we read where Abel, a nice guy, offered an acceptable gift to God as an act of devotion. Doing the right thing did not prevent his death by the hands of his jealous brother.

The promises of God do not depend upon victorious validation by earthly standards. The emerging experience of God's transforming presence sustains faith defined as *"the assurance of things hoped for and the conviction of things unseen."* Faith is a journey from a world of things that can be known and managed to *"an inheritance"* that is promised and envisioned, even though it presently is *"seen through a glass darkly, but then face to face."*

Standing on the promises of Christ the Lord,
Bound to him eternally by love's strong cord,
Overcoming daily with the Spirit's sword,
Standing on the promises of God.
—*R. Kelso Carter*

BEHAVIOR IS THE LANGUAGE OF FAITH!

Goodness And Justice
Isaiah 1:10-17

Viewed as chosen and blessed, the Jews had an obligation under the covenant to reflect God's influence upon both their institutional and personal lives. Isaiah made plain God's displeasure in a split-covenanted life. He publicly lamented the powerful inclination of God's chosen to develop and structure their religious institutions to accommodate social convenience while neglecting the purpose of their special calling to do good and seek justice in God's name. He came down hard against institutional religion with its emphasis upon matters of secondary importance to their original covenant with God.

It is inadequate for God's purpose to ritualize words of goodness and justice while ignoring human adversity. Like a narcotic, the purpose of form without substance is to provide euphoria. The prophet challenges his hearers to rediscover and recommit to daily social application of God's blessing given to them to pass on.

Receiving an undeserved gift can be a problem unless there is a clear understanding of the conditions involved in giving and receiving. The receiver must know that he is not expected to perform to the magnitude of the gift. Rather, inadequacy needs to be acknowledged as a precondition if the gift is to become a means of shared improvement. One might relate the gift of God's blessings to a gift membership in a Fitness Gym where inadequacy is a constant challenge and improvement is a constant incentive. The assistance and encouragement of other members are needed and graciously provided. The gym is furnished with weight benches, not lounge chairs.

> Let not conscience make you linger,
> Nor of fitness fondly dream;
> All the fitness he required
> Is to feel your need of him;
> This he gives you,
> This he gives you;
> 'Tis the Spirits glimmering beam.
> —Joseph Hart

"I Am"

Exodus 3:7-22

For practical purposes, if we can't name it, it doesn't exist. Moses was realistic to ask for an authoritative name before he confronted the oppressive governmental and religious powers of Egypt to demand freedom for enslaved Israelites. Both master and slave demanded authentic evidence before implementing drastic change. God's response to Moses establishes, once and for all in Biblical literature, that God prefers to remain nameless. He is known only through his influence. God is event-oriented rather than word-oriented. This made it natural for Jesus to teach with parables rather than abstract philosophical concepts.

Sharing a religious experience is valuable because God is credited with being the originator. There is no necessity to analyze or to establish methods that attempt to reproduce results objectively. The community of faith responds individually and collectively to divine presence. The results, over time, validate or invalidate authenticity.

The Bible refers to God as the *"one who delivered the children of Israel from the house of bondage."* The power that effected the change is given a name that references the change. Had Moses not acted upon God's influence, and had the Israelites not responded to his leadership, there would be no power known as *"the one who delivered..."* Generations later, Jesus would say to Nicodemus, who came to him in the night with religious questions, *"You must be born again..."* where behavior, not words, is the language of children and the language of faith.

To all, life thou givest, to both great and small;
In all life thou livest, the true life of all;
We blossom and flourish as leaves on the tree,
And wither and perish, but naught changeth thee.
—*Walter Chalmers Smith*

Building Up One's Neighbor
Romans 15:1-13

Inequity is one of life's accepted constants. Although we apparently originate from a common primitive gene source, the likeness quickly fractures into obvious inequities. The fundamental inequity put on regular display in the Bible is between the strong and the weak.

It is significant that Jesus embodied the power of God to address a variety of circumstances involving those who are weak. Paul plainly instructed the church in Rome that those who proclaim the power of compassion are expected to *"put up with"* the failing of the weak for the greater purpose of **"glorifying God."**

The world is astonished and is all ears any time power pauses to address need. Minimizing disparity is a pathway to greater harmony. However, through such effort, people of faith are "standing on the promises of Christ our King."

From Thee all skill and science flow,
All pity, care and love,
All calm and courage, faith and hope:
O pour them from above;
And part them Lord, to each and all,
As each and all shall need,
To rise, like incense, each to Thee,
In noble thought and deed.
—*Charles Kingsley*

BEHAVIOR IS THE LANGUAGE OF FAITH!

New Covenant
Jeremiah 31:23-34

Jeremiah attributes both adversity and blessing to God. In the world of cause and effect, he looked upon adversity as preparation for blessing. Arrogance requires breaking down before one is receptive to developing qualities that are worthy of God's blessing.

The idea didn't originate with Jeremiah. Refer to the creation story in Genesis wherein arrogant disobedience of Adam and Eve resulted in a future of adversity, struggle, and pain. The consequence of disobedience is not vindictive punishment. Rather, it is a program for attitude adjustment designed to cultivate humility before God.

God made a covenant of obedience with Jeremiah's religious community. Laws governing and promoting acceptable conduct were provided as a self-help program for attaining life that pleases God. The Law emphasizes knowledge and teaching. This appears to be an appealing approach. Failure to bring about desired results is supposed to motivate turning to God for deliverance. God patiently waits for this to happen.

Jeremiah recognized that the Covenant of Law was limited because it became one more demonstration of human arrogance rather than an avenue for humility. He predicted a new covenant of humility to replace the self-help covenant of arrogance, wherein *"God will write upon our hearts, from the least to the greatest."*

> We by his spirit prove
> And know the things of God,
> The things which freely of his love
> He hath on us bestowed.
> —*Charles Wesley*

Leadership
I Samuel 18:1-5

D avid, a poor shepherd, was elevated by King Saul to a position of military responsibility because of his courage and independence. Saul's son Jonathan and David were devoted friends, and, he, along with *"all the people, even the servants of Saul, approved"* of David's position of leadership.

According to the Biblical account, David killed Goliath with a stone and a sling and advanced from a poor shepherd to military prominence. When Saul's army wanted to retreat before the mighty Philistines, David said, *"The Lord, who saved me from the paw of the lion and from the paw of the bear, will save me from the hand of this Philistine."* David's confidence was based upon his success in defeating wild beasts in the hills where he tended sheep. His envisioned victory over Goliath was based upon experience.

Two things about David that captured Saul's attention were Jonathan's affection and the people's approval. The story of David's defeat of Goliath directs us to visualize success resulting from the spontaneous confident behavior of a shepherd boy who based his actions on past reliance upon God that produced favorable results. In contrast, the battle plans of a king and his generals dissolved in fear before a more powerful adversary. David's place in history was secured.

What is the focal point of David's success story? Behavior, that is the language of children, is also the language of faith. Words attempt analysis and evaluation, but behavior communicates feelings that words cannot express. *God communicates with the world through the sensitive behavior of the community of faith.*

O for a faith that will not shrink,
Though pressed by every foe,
That will not tremble brink
Of any earthly woe.
—*William H. Bathurst*

All Things To All People
I Corinthians 9:15-23

Diversity is a generally accepted characteristic of religion. It exists within, and between, religions. So, which one is right? Probing for the lowest common denominator is an exercise for people interested in comparative religions, but few people are gratified by a consensus religion.

All religions have a word with which they refer to deity, but there is no common experience or perception of divine characteristics. Everything has to have a name if it is going to be discussed. The apostle Paul utilizes this broad base to characterize God as one who exercises love and power, both of which were demonstrated in the life of Jesus. Religion in abstract is limited. Therefore, the New Testament says that God revealed in Jesus the structure that reveals divine purpose and serves the common good. With the term *"all things to all people,"* Paul put a shot across the bow of any spiritual ship sailing with an exclusive cargo of personal salvation. He knew from experience how important it was to eliminate any basis in Christian faith for individual boasting.

Come ye that love the Lord,
And let your joys be known;
Join in a song with sweet accord,
While ye surround his throne.
—*Isaac Watts*

BEHAVIOR IS THE LANGUAGE OF FAITH!

A Sketch And A Shadow
Hebrews 8:1-12

The construction of a church is preceded by design, plan, and an occasional scale model; yet, the project might or might not be constructed as designed. The architect, building committee, and congregation must have a meeting of the minds before the first shovel of dirt is turned. Anything less has little chance of completion. Similarly, Paul described God's covenant with the Jews as a plan not fully accepted as prepared. He referred to this covenant as *"a sketch and shadow"* placed in the narthex of institutional Temple religion. Without a meeting of the minds, this covenant was not implemented.

God responded with a new covenant that appeals directly to those who need it. He put this new plan in the mind and heart of those who accept it. The old plan became subordinate. The past is forgiven. God's new plan is known from the *"least to the greatest,"* and it is communicated to the world more accurately through the behavioral language of faith rather than the reasoned words of admirers.

Thou art the Way, the Truth, the Life;
Grant us that way to know,
That truth to keep, that life to win,
Whose joys eternal flow.
—*George W. Doane*

BEHAVIOR IS THE LANGUAGE OF FAITH!

Anticipation
Luke 12:35-40

Christianity is a religion of hope. Gratification through material benefits is viewed as secondary to incomparable deferred blessings that come from God to those who value justice, kindness, and humility before God. The poetic words of Psalm 37:16, 30-31 say, *"Better is the little that a righteous person has than the abundance of the many wicked."*

"The mouths of the righteous utter wisdom, and their tongues speak justice. The Law of their God is in their heart: Their steps do not slip..."

One cannot take righteousness, justice, and a God-conscious heart to the bank. These qualities, though occasionally admired by humanity, do not satisfy the senses or produce currency for deposit. The hope and promises of Christian faith are fantasy when they are tales told by others, but they are reality when they become the marks by which one sets a course and sails life's hazardous waters.

> But we never can prove
> The delights of his love
> Until all on the altar we lay;
> For the favor he shows,
> And the joy he bestows
> Are for them who will
> Trust and obey.
> —*John H. Sammis*

BEHAVIOR IS THE LANGUAGE OF FAITH!

Strengthened By Grace
Hebrews 13:1-21

This is Paul's letter to a Christian community that he founded; one that was experiencing brutal persecution. He wanted this small cluster of sufferers to be strong and to maintain a Godly attitude toward others. The teacher began by reminding them to demonstrate toward strangers, within the community of believers, the love that is extended to one's family members. This was followed with particular instructions regarding one's marriage partner, leaders whose deeds are honorable, and those in need.

One warning was sounded concerning money, which he said should be managed, not loved as a primary motivator. Unconditional love is expressed only as evidence of God's grace; it is empowered by God and is not to be frivolously misapplied.

Love among family members motivates behavior that contrasts to laws, codes, and regulations that are designed to provide an orderly and reliable environment for creative living.

Unconditional love overflows from the reservoir of God's grace freely and generously poured into the feelings and thoughts of those who need and desire it.

Behavior, the language of faith, usually needs no explanation, whereas rules call for explanation. Paul summarizes with the reminder to **"do good"** and to *"share."* Both of these are applicable from kindergarten to retirement home. The details are a challenge for which we need God's grace.

> I find, I walk, I love, but oh, the whole
> Of love is but my answer, Lord to thee!
> For thou wert long beforehand with my soul;
> Always, thou lovedst me.
> —*Anonymous,* The Pilgrim Hymnal

Kingdom At Hand
Matthew 10:1-15

The disciples were summoned, commissioned, empowered, and given priorities. Their message was, *"The kingdom of God is near."* On first blush, the "for Jews only" restriction in Matthew's Gospel appears inconsistent with the universality with which we associate the ministry of Jesus.

Upon further reflection, we see that the birth of Jesus, the location of his ministry, and his ethnic origin are significant practical limitations upon his universal purpose. It is worth acknowledging that practical limitations are utilized consistently throughout history as the context in which God reveals his purpose.

Beginning with Abraham's response to Sacred Presence, history prepared the Jews to serve as the reasonable first choice among world religions to immediately understand and respond to Jesus' message concerning the kingdom of God. Had they responded positively to Jesus, they would have provided an instant cadre of well-instructed people to proclaim God's kingdom. When the most qualified decline the opportunity, God calls and trains others to serve His purpose.

A charge to keep I have,
A God to glorify,
A never dying soul to save,
And fit it for the sky.
—*Charles Wesley*

BEHAVIOR IS THE LANGUAGE OF FAITH!

Patient Endurance
Luke 8:4-15

The Parable of the Sower describes characteristics of hot and cold commitment. The word pictures are clear and most people can differentiate between those with limited enthusiasm and those who are *"bearing fruit"* with *"patient endurance."*

We must avoid the temptation to look upon *"good soil"* as a moral precondition that enables some to *"bring forth grain"* while others cannot. All need repentance and forgiveness that are the duel plows which break through the hard crust of neglect and prepare for seeds of transformation that *"bear fruit"* through behavior that is the true language of faith.

Let us not neglect the last two words of the parable, *"patient endurance."* Look at the message from back to front and see that the most desperate need is for others to observe people of faith *"bearing fruit"* with *"patient endurance."* Time is too precious to devote large chunks to analyzing failed efforts. Knowing what fails is important, but it is no substitute for **"patiently enduring"** difficulties while going about doing what we are convinced is for the common good and the glory of God. Endurance is necessary when testing is inevitable and unrelenting.

A cloud of witnesses around
Holds thee in full survey;
Forget the steps already trod,
And onward urge thy way.
—*Philip Doddridge*

BEHAVIOR IS THE LANGUAGE OF FAITH!

Sending You
Matthew 10:16-20

C hristianity is a religion of shared faith. Faith is analogous to a lockbox containing valued possessions that require two keys in the hands of two individuals who must be present when the box is unlocked. Faith is personal, but its value is accessed only when shared.

Personal values are not necessarily of interest to others. However, shared faith values can be appreciated, tolerated, or rejected. Jesus warned people of faith to be aware of those who are antagonized and become hostile and cruel because of Christian behavior.

Jesus called upon his followers to share the power to love that serves the common good. Personal power, focused upon personal advantage and permanent gain, is threatened by the concept of common good. History validates Jesus' prediction of cruel persecution of those who seek the common good. Faith that gives witness to a power shift from personal gratification to common good results from firm commitment and divine influence.

Yield to me now, for I am weak,
But confident in self-despair;
Speak to my heart, in blessing speak,
Be conquered by my instant prayer;
Speak, or thou never hence shalt move,
And tell me if thy name is love.
—*Charles Wesley*

I Am With You
Isaiah 41:1-10

The *"blessed assurance,"* to which Christians attest, is anchored in silence because God has a history of not speaking when others are speaking. When God does speak, humans have a track record of interrupting with long monologues. Those who are wise develop the ability to *"listen in silence"* to the Creator who gives life and takes it back. As the Bible teaches, *"I, the Lord, am first, and will be with the last."* Grammarians and artisans have always been able to fashion words and objects that give expression to religious intuition. As wonderful as they are, they cannot substitute for every person's need to know that he or she is being addressed by the One in Control. Isaiah reminds his listeners that God has chosen them to serve Him based upon the inner assurance that *"I am with you."* God cannot be handled, put in an appropriate place, or conveniently dismissed. Frequently, the habit of refusing to listen produces unpleasant results. However, to those who *"listen in silence,"* God's presence is strength and help. He upholds His servants.

> I ask no dream, no prophet ecstasies,
> No sudden rending of the veil of clay,
> No angel visitant, no opening skies;
> But take the dimness of my soul away.
> —*George Caroly*

BEHAVIOR IS THE LANGUAGE OF FAITH!

Weak And Strong
I Corinthians 11:7-12:10

We promote self-esteem because it is important for creative high-quality well-being. Paul distinguishes between desirable self-esteem and undesirable arrogance. For him, arrogance is puffed up, boastful, and makes us feel that we are a superior kind. Pride is inconsistent with the servant role that Jesus adopted as the model for his followers.

Paul's personal redemptive experience convinced him that there was nothing about himself that obligated God to effect such an extreme change in his life. In his view, arrogance and boasting were not possible for those who know that God is due the honor and public acclaim. Paul's behavior is a living testimony that deeds of loving service are empowered by God and require no self-serving explanation.

O what a blessed hope is ours!
While here on earth we stay.
We more than taste the heavenly powers,
And antedate that day;
We feel the resurrection near,
Our life in Christ concealed,
And with his glorious presence here
Our earthen vessels filled.
—*Charles Wesley*

BEHAVIOR IS THE LANGUAGE OF FAITH!

Concessions
Mark 10:1-12

The Pharisees asked Jesus, *"Is it lawful for a man to divorce his wife?"* Note, they didn't reference a woman divorcing her husband because women in that time and culture were not unilaterally allowed that option. Biblical culture and legal system were male dominated. Women were treated similar to possessions and were kept or disposed of at the discretion of men. The primary function of women was to receive male sperm, produce offspring of male linage, and nurture them to maturity. Even righteousness and sin were generally viewed as transmitted through male sperm. Hence, we read about propagation of the "sins of Adam" being canceled and overcome by the grace of God through faith in Jesus, the **"second Adam."**

Bible study is enhanced when we put forth the effort to transfer our categories of understanding into the culture of the time. Male and female relations, as all sexual acts, were evaluated based upon sex that resulted in a child, preferably a male child. The story in Genesis concerning Lot's daughters is about getting him drunk so he would engage in incest with them and fulfill their lives by perpetuating his seed. A barren woman was an unfulfilled life without purpose; the same as bestiality, homosexuality, masturbation, etc., all of which were considered an affront to God who wanted productivity.

Jesus told the Pharisees that Moses made provisions for a man to divorce his wife because of male *"hard heartedness"* that placed male ego gratification and public status above unproductive sex. Although it isn't addressed here, female concubines and servants also served men as baby factories, and they were evaluated according to their productivity.

Jesus deconstructed thousands of years of male dominance in marriage by saying, *"the two shall become one flesh... therefore, what God has joined together let no one separate."* Jesus did not rescind the concession of Moses regarding divorce because *"hardness of heart"* persists. This is one more example of how Jesus emphasizes the need for a transformed heart, influenced by sacred presence that exceeds the Law of the Scribes and the Pharisees.

These things shall be: a loftier race
Than e'er the world hath known shall rise
With flame of freedom in their souls
And light of knowledge in their eyes.
—*Addington Symonds*

BEHAVIOR IS THE LANGUAGE OF FAITH!

"Wash Your Heart"
Jeremiah 4:5-18

The Bible teaches that humanity prefers a self-portrait over creation in the likeness of God. The Creator permits the alternative that exposes human limitations. The creative process has a built-in default system that consistently destroys any human effort to permanently alter the plan designed to glorify the Creator through serving the common good. Abraham is portrayed as a chosen prototype blessed by God in order to be a blessing to others.

Refusal to find a method to share blessings doesn't require a moment of rage because God put default corrective countermeasures in place in the beginning. Adam and Eve were forewarned of the prohibitions and the consequences for not following the plan. Genesis tells us that the negative consequences of disobedience infected humanity like a savage virus that displaced shared blessings. Jeremiah's message to

God's chosen people, who were in the throes of corrective countermeasures, was: *"Your ways and your doings have brought this upon you. This is your doom; how bitter it is! It has reached your very heart."*

God's judgment against arrogant animosity and destruction is not sporadic. Over five hundred years after Jeremiah, Jesus said, *"...for I did not come to judge the world but to save the world. He who rejects me and does not receive my words has a Judge..."* The Creator's unrelenting desire is to salvage and restore to good use all that is judged and condemned. With this eternal truth in mind, Jeremiah delivered the message, *"Wash your heart clean of wickedness so that you may be saved..."* and serve the good purpose for which you were created.

> Place on the Lord reliance;
> My soul with courage wait;
> His truth be thine affiance,
> When faint and desolate.
> His might thy heart shall strengthen,
> His love thy joy increase;
> Mercy thy days shall lengthen;
> The Lord will give thee peace.
> —James Montgomery

Chosen And Blest
Deuteronomy 7:6-14

Those who believe in God tend to view events during their lifetime as tailor-made for them. Historically, this cultural mindset is overwhelmed by God's redemptive love and righteous judgment that are free of cultural bias. It is important to feel and understand that God is the creating, influential, judging, and redeeming force in every age. Otherwise, arrogance and colloquialism become hindrances to mature spiritual development.

Experience in the womb makes it natural for a child to think and feel singly important. Adults are never free from that initial impression. It is an ever-present challenge to counteract that effect. How we manage the challenge is culture-coded, and what we do affects the common good within a social environment of continuous testing. The Bible records thousands of years of selected human responses to God's creative presence. Those responses provide us with an assortment of cross-cultural opportunities to learn how to serve a true and living God.

> God send us men whose aim 'twill be
> Not to defend some ancient creed,
> But to live out the laws of Christ
> In every thought and word and deed.
> —*Frederick J. Gillman*

BEHAVIOR IS THE LANGUAGE OF FAITH!

Servants And Stewards
II Corinthians 4:1-6

Servants and slaves acted without question upon the instructions of their master. Paul finds that this relationship provided the most accurate comparison to the relationship between Jesus and his followers. Nothing more completely projected the image of total control. Servants and slaves were not part-time. Full-time commitment to assigned tasks was expected. The master of the household exercised sole authority to pass judgment because he alone had access to, and knowledge of, all the particulars.

Paul was content to leave judgment to the "risen Lord" who knows the purposes of the heart. Everyone else employs clumsy hit-and-miss attempts to put motive and action together for temporary performance evaluation. It is worth noting that Judgment is more serious than performance evaluation. Judgment is final, and, thankfully, is God's call to make. Performance evaluation is ongoing as we *"work out our own salvation with fear and trembling."*

> Other refuge have I none;
> Hangs my helpless soul on thee;
> Leave, ah! Leave me not alone,
> Still support and comfort me.
> All my trust on thee is stayed;
> All my help from thee I bring;
> Cover my defenseless head
> With the shadow of thy wing.
> —*Charles Wesley*

BEHAVIOR IS THE LANGUAGE OF FAITH!

Special Utensils
II Timothy 2:14-26

Aknowledgeable and committed worker can achieve superior performance when minimum time is used in procedural discussions. Paul applies this commonsense observation to Christians quarreling over theological perceptions to the neglect of practical issues related to immediate needs.

Paul compared quarreling factions within the fellowship to common ordinary household utensils. More appropriately, the community of faith should reflect high quality. The Lord's servants are called to be *"special utensils"* because of the *"good work"* they perform.

What did Paul present as the characteristics of a good worker? *"Righteousness, faith, love, peace, and calling to God with a pure heart."* Christian discipleship means less talk and more activity. John Wesley is said to have offered this brief reminder of Christian priorities—simplicity (one design) and purity (one desire) focused upon entire devotion to God.

Through him the first fond prayers are said,
Our lips of childhood frame;
The last low whispers of our dead
Are burdened with his name.
—*John Greenleaf Whittier*

BEHAVIOR IS THE LANGUAGE OF FAITH!

Holiness And Humility
Isaiah 57:1-21

God is flexible. From His elevated and incomprehensible position He bends low and touches the lives of those who know that they do not know. As one who *"dwells in a high and holy place,"* He enters the thoughts of the humble and overwhelms knowledge and understanding.

He bends down to lift up those who are otherwise hopelessly bogged down in the limited existence of sensible things that can be seen, touched, smelled, heard, and tasted. He understands and is patient with the response time to His influential presence.

The prophet says that God episodically and painfully permits us to be corrected in order to focus our attention upon His enduring presence. Those who ignore or tranquilize the pain are destined to remain within the unenlightened cocoon they design and construct.

God be in my head, and in my understanding;
God be in my eyes, and in my looking;
God be in my mouth, and in my speaking;
God be in my heart, and in my thinking;
God be at my end, and at my departing.
—*Henry Walford Davies*

BEHAVIOR IS THE LANGUAGE OF FAITH!

Inescapable God
Psalm 139

God is inescapable. His enduring presence **"hems us in."** God-knowledge is limited and frustrating. We habitually associate knowledge with some degree of control. However, God cannot be managed. The Psalmist says, **"He is too wonderful for me."**

The natural inclination is to put out of mind anything we cannot comprehend or manage. However, God remains on the scene in moments of spiritual ecstasy and in decisions of denial. The Creator **"formed our inward parts and knit them together in our *mother's* womb,"** resulting in a *"fearfully and wonderfully made"* product. God's thoughts are not naturally our thoughts. Yet, *"we are still with him."*

Exasperated by our limitations, we pray with the Psalmist, *"Search us and know our hearts, test us and know our thoughts, and lead us in the way everlasting."* It is not important that we are all-knowing. It is important that God is all-knowing.

> O love that wilt not let me go,
> I rest my weary soul in thee;
> I give thee back the life I owe,
> That in thine ocean depths its flow
> May richer, fuller be.
> —*George Matheson*

BEHAVIOR IS THE LANGUAGE OF FAITH!

Obligations
Romans 13

Paul tells the Christian community in Rome about their God-given responsibility to honor just obligations to the state as well as to love one another. Social and personal orderliness are features of God's design.

The Roman government provided safety and freedom of movement for its subjects throughout the empire while having no interest in religious beliefs and practices that did not challenge their authority. Paul's Roman citizenship enabled him to avoid abuse and possible execution by local tribunals. He felt that a legal system such as this should be supported by taxes, revenue, respect, and honor as *"its' due."* Support should result from good conscience not fear of punishment.

Governments impose standards for social behavior with unpleasant consequences for violators. Within the context of this basic order, Christians are called to the higher standard of *"Love your neighbor as yourself."* Love for others is a calling that satisfies both secular and religious laws designed to contain the negative consequences of human depravity. The power to love that comes from God provides added value that more gracefully serves the common good.

Not alone for mighty empire,
Stretching far o'er land and sea,
Not alone for bounteous harvests,
Lift we up our hearts to thee:
Standing in the living present,
Memory and hope between,
Lord, we would with deep thanksgiving,
Praise thee most for things unseen.
—*William P. Merrill*

Nothing Left Over
Exodus 16:1-21

The relationship between Creator and created is presented in verse fourteen of the one hundred sixth Psalm *"...They had a wonton craving in the wilderness and put God to the test."* We have a bundle of cravings. Our ability to manage them is tested because each one presents a mass of gratification that cannot be ignored. Moral fiber is affected by the way we prioritize desires. We *"test God"* when we appeal to Him as a means of satisfying our cravings.

It's important to be aware that God's approach to management of gratification is related to need, not excess. Excess enters the scene as our test for how well we manage abundance. There is no established plan for managing excess because every system is vulnerable to exploitation for personal gain rather than serving God's interest in the common good.

The community of believers, individually and collectively, must constantly and prayerfully devise and revise the plan for managing excess in response to need. The test is unchanged. The answers are written on our hearts, free from the threat of bootlegging.

"Word of the ever-living God,
Will of his glorious Son:
Without thee how could earth be trod,
Or heaven itself be won?"
—*Bernard Barton*

BEHAVIOR IS THE LANGUAGE OF FAITH!

More Than Conquerors
Romans 8:37-39

Conquests usually result from skillful use of power and tactics. Results are always temporary because victory has built-in obsolescence wherein sooner or later more powerful and more tactical conquerors come and destroy.

First-century Jews were born into a world dominated by Roman conquest and rule, resulting in Temple destruction and population dispersion. It was to these Jewish Christians that Paul wrote words of assurance that, unlike conquerors of power and tactic, their victory is permanent because it is God's gift of love made known through the life and teachings of Jesus.

Such a victory is a matter of relationships of love and devotion, not geographical or institutional control. Culture continues to provide the structure, but not the limit, for expressing our response to the Creator, Who seeks to tailor an effective relationship with each of us that is not limited by time, place, or circumstance. Be mindful that tailor-made personal arrangements require more time and effort than ready-made and massed produced, **"For he knows how we were made; he remembers that we are dust."** (Psalm 103:14)

Thanks to God whose Word is answered
By the Spirit's voice within.
Here we drink of joy unmeasured,
Life redeemed from death and sin.
God is speaking; God is speaking;
Praise Him for his open Word.
—*R.T. Brooks*

God's Appeal
II Corinthians 5:16-21

Reconciled to God, we no longer regard others *"from a human point of view."* This means criteria for evaluating others is no longer based upon endless combinations of personal preferences and prejudices. We view everyone from Christ's vantage point on the cross *"Father forgive them for they know not what they do."* No one is trashed, although some show more promise than others.

Christians have an unlimited marketplace in which to demonstrate the meaning of reconciliation to God. Words and deeds establish the unnatural attitude that we no longer *"regard others from a human point of view,"* even though that is the way most prefer to be viewed. It is unrealistic to expect accommodation in an environment where justice, righteousness, and the common good are subordinated to personal power and control. Paul tells us that reconciliation to God, expressed through our daily activities, is evidence that *"we become the righteousness of God."*

AWESOME teaching!!

> Come ye weary, heavy laden,
> Bruised and mangled from the fall;
> If you tarry till you're better,
> You will never come at all;
> Not the righteous; not the righteous,
> Sinners Jesus came to call
> —*Joseph Hart*

BEHAVIOR IS THE LANGUAGE OF FAITH!

Embarrassed Creator
Ezekiel 36:22-32

E zekiel was prophet to a conquered people who were deported from their homeland to a life of servitude in a foreign land. Years of captivity resulted in adoption of the gods of their conquerors to the neglect of the God of their fathers. Ezekiel pointed out that this devotional change resulted in unclean and destructive habits that reflected poorly upon the God of their ancestors.

Ezekiel repeatedly emphasized to his people that God's response to this embarrassment was motivation to clear His holy name. God did not want to be associated with the destructive changes that were taking place. It is especially interesting to see how Ezekiel underscored God's interest in serving His own purpose and benefit rather than establish intervention upon the unreliability and unworthiness of those whom He reliably accompanied into captivity.

He began recovering his reputation through a rehabilitation process that cleansed the hearts of the unfaithful so that *"his holiness might again be displayed through them."* He *"removed their heart of stone"* and **"gave them a new heart ...and put his spirit in** *them.***"** This observable transformation intended to signal all nations that the *"glory of God"* was the solitary factor that could possibly account for such a remarkable change.

God of the earth, the sky, the sea,
Maker of all above, below,
Creation lives and moves in thee,
Thy present life, through all doth flow.
—*Samuel Longfellow*

BEHAVIOR IS THE LANGUAGE OF FAITH!

Bearing Fruit
Colossians 1:1-8

The "power words" currently demonstrated among Colossian Christians are: faith, love, hope, and truth. They are the foundation blocks upon which the Christian community is built. Paul also emphasized, **"bearing fruit, growing, comprehending, and *grace.*"** These words bring together thoughts and feelings that demonstrate value. The Creator influences us physically and spiritually. He graciously makes his will known to us at levels of awareness that we are able to experience individually.

God also tests for quality and effectiveness. Unpleasant as it is, He utilizes a full-time Tester. The Bible details specific events such as those notoriously experienced by Job and Jesus. They plainly demonstrate the system. Scientific and spiritual testing are valuable because they demonstrate what is, and is not, effective. Everything in God's universe is being arranged to serve His eternal purpose.

With a child's glad heart of love
At thy bidding may I move,
Prompt to serve and follow thee,
Loving him who first loved me.
—*Jane E. Leeson*

BEHAVIOR IS THE LANGUAGE OF FAITH!

Sleeper Awake
Ephesians 5:1-20

Paul contrasts unenlightened and destructive attitudes and activities with those that are creative and worthy of public praise and thanksgiving. The secret life of the children of darkness might be compared to a sleepwalker to whom God says, *"Sleeper awake."*

Children of light are distinguished by *"fruit of the light"* for which they are able to thank God. Awakened from sleep, time becomes too valuable to waste. Children of light are able to do things openly. They thank God for the desire and the opportunity to bear fruit that is worth sharing *"in the name of our Lord Jesus Christ."*

> Direct, control, suggest, this day,
> All design, or do, or say,
> That all my powers, with all their might,
> In Thy sole glory may unite.
> —*Thomas Ken*

BEHAVIOR IS THE LANGUAGE OF FAITH!

Prophets And Jesus
Revelation 9:1-10

Religion that is limited to rules and memorials is impersonal and is subject to institutional rigidity. In contrast the comfortable relationship that Jesus had with God made formality irrelevant and enabled him to refer to the

Giver of Life as Father. There is rejoicing in heaven because the Heavenly Father communicates to the world through the Law, Prophets, Jesus, and the community of faith.

God, the one *"high and lifted up,"* who was veiled behind the curtain of separation and the cloud of unknowing, became the man Jesus, who traveled the dusty dirty roads of Galilee. Jesus illustrated how important it is that he never *"thought of himself more highly than he ought to think,"* but presented himself as *"humble and obedient servant."* He was unjustly killed, but justly resurrected by our Heavenly Father who credits the righteousness of Jesus to those who seek him and follow his lead. This is cause for celebration.

He speaks, and listening to his voice,
New life the dead receive.
The mournful, broken hearts rejoice;
The humble poor believe.
—*Charles Wesley*

BEHAVIOR IS THE LANGUAGE OF FAITH!

Fear And Faith
Exodus 14:19-31

An underemphasized Biblical proclamation is that **"the fear of God is the beginning of wisdom."** Our meditation scripture presents a scene that reasonably evoked fear when natural things acted exceedingly unnatural. We are reminded that the Creator of the universe is powerful and is capable of manipulating the natural order for destruction or preservation. Even nonbelievers are reminded of their mortality when they stand in awe and fear of the natural order being disorderly.

Although *"the heavens declare the glory of God and the firmament showeth his handiwork,"* Moses needed divinely-authorized commandments to attempt formation of an orderly social environment. The commandments, with consequences for disobedience, are based upon fear. They have limited value because communal observance of laws typically run in cycles that begin with strict adherence and gradually modify because of habitually delayed, diluted, or ignored consequences. Over time, fear subsides and observance becomes ceremonial. Rediscovery and re-emphasis of the law typically follows an intolerable erosion of quality human relationships.

The Gospel of Luke reports angel voices, at the birth of Jesus, proclaiming, **"Fear not, for, behold, you I bring good tidings of great joy..."** The arrival of Jesus supersedes the law of fear with which we began and replaces it with a relationship of forgiveness, redemption, and the power to love, against which there is no law. Appropriate response is gratitude.

Grant unto us communion with thee,
Thou star abiding one;
Come unto us and dwell with us;
With thee are found the gifts of life,
Bless us with life that has no end,
Eternal life with thee.
—*American Folk Hymn,* paraphrase by Philip Frazier

Faithful And Tested

II Thessalonians 2-3

This is personal correspondence from Paul, delivered by Timothy, to the community of faith in Thessalonica. Paul was concerned that persecution and suffering for their faithfulness would cause them to drift away. He reminded them of the hardships of faith endured by other people of faith, including the Old Testament prophets.

Paul reminded them that his time in their community was characterized by good conduct without personal gain; rather, with emphasis upon gentleness, caring, sharing, and pleading on behalf of God's word. In spite of his warning, Paul worried that the Tempter's harsh conditions would shake their convictions.

The good news Timothy brought back to Paul reaffirmed the faith and love of the community of believers in Thessalonica. It strengthened Paul's faith and gave him joy. Christian faith lives in and through the communion of believers who share the good news, the good life, and the hope of victory over the Tempter. God is glorified.

> Thou bidst us go with thee to stand
> Against hell's marshaled powers;
> And heart to heart and hand to hand,
> To make thine honor ours.
> —Ray Palmer

BEHAVIOR IS THE LANGUAGE OF FAITH!

Madness
Acts 26:1-29

The death and resurrection of Jesus for the redemption of unworthy humanity is madness to all except those for whom it is a personal experience. The presence of God is a developing influence that is authenticated through altered behavior as the primary language of faith. Like the blind man healed by Jesus, explanations are limited to: *"All I know is, I was blind but now I see."*

What we have felt and seen
With confidence we tell;
And publish to the sons of men
The signs infallible.
—*Charles Wesley*

BEHAVIOR IS THE LANGUAGE OF FAITH!

Sower And Reaper
John 4:31-38

Can there be any possible misperception about the communal nature of the Christian gospel? Personal pronouns are not the most appropriate or enlightened words for communicating the *"good news."* There is no basis for personal accolades because the process dwarfs individual involvement that is naturally limited by time and capability.

Jesus emphasized the communal focus of the Christian message when he said, *"God does not wish that any of his children should be lost."* The communal dimension of the gospel is missing when the message revolves around personal elaboration. Jesus said that his purpose was to do the *"will of his Father."* Paul took up the theme when he wrote, *"Whatever I count as gain for myself is lost for Christ."* One wonders how personal salvation gained such a foothold in Christian theology.

The community of faith must take care not to drift into self-righteousness or theological arrogance where *"Satan lies close at the doorstep."* Our time is brief and our talents are limited, but we can all plant the seed of common good that we have in hand with the conviction that God controls the harvest.

> To give and give, and give again,
> What God hath given thee;
> To spread thyself nor count the cost,
> To serve right gloriously
> The God who gave all worlds that are,
> And all that are to be.
> —G.A. Studdert-Kennedy

BEHAVIOR IS THE LANGUAGE OF FAITH!

Household Divided
Luke 12:35-59

Jesus' message of redemption, transformation, and peace is proclaimed and practiced in a hostile environment. The likelihood of conflict is a reality that turns off many potential followers. This is especially the case in light of Jesus' warning that households can become divided over him and his message. Can anyone doubt the intensity of such conflict?

Religion has been the basis for some of the most divisive and destructive conflicts in human history. The intensity appears greatest among those who are religious, rather than between the religious and the nonreligious. We are reminded that in this environment we cannot afford to develop sloppy ways of thinking and acting that compromise our primary purpose. There is no certainty that we will have time to clean up a mess before we die. Jesus made it plain that he expects his followers to remain *"faithful and prudent"* managers of that with which they have been entrusted, even in times of conflict.

"I would be true, for there are those who trust me;
I would be pure, for there are those who care;
I would be strong, for there is much to suffer;
I would be brave, for there is much to dare."
—*Howard A. Walter*

BEHAVIOR IS THE LANGUAGE OF FAITH!

Count Wisely
Psalm 90

The Creator's sphere of influence is from *"everlasting to everlasting."* In contrast, everything we experience is measured, although everyone does not deal with the same measure. Commonality is found in the dust from which we came and to which we return as *"our years come to an end like a sigh."*

We would be wise to regularly ask God to *"teach us to count our days that we may gain a wise heart."* Otherwise, we may repetitively squander and rehabilitate our measured moments. We pray with the Psalmist that *"the work of our hands prosper"* because we know that a lifetime of effort cannot be deleted and redone.

Thanks be to God whose deep compassion and immeasurable time enables our *"brief sigh"* to serve his everlasting meaning and purpose, or, *"What is humanity that you are mindful of it?"* Jesus served with a *"wise heart,"* as he counted his days to the benefit of humanity and to the glory of God.

O what a blessed hope is ours!
While here on earth we stay.
We more than taste the heavenly powers,
And antedate that day;
We feel the resurrection near,
Our life in Christ concealed,
And with his glorious presence here
His life in us revealed.
—*Charles Wesley*

BEHAVIOR IS THE LANGUAGE OF FAITH!

Believe
John 11:1-44

Resurrection from the dead is the foundation of Christian faith. Nothing else can give permanency to life and glorify God who creates and perpetuates it. Paul emphasized: *"If Christ be not raised from the dead, our faith is in vain."* Without resurrection we are left with, *"eat drink and be merry for tomorrow you may die."*

Resurrection is an exceptional act of God comparable to *"In the beginning God created..."* For a clearer understanding, contrast resurrection (a special act of God) with immortality (uninterrupted existence exclusive to God). Paul acknowledges this essential difference when he said of humans, **"this mortal (subject to death) shall put on immortality (gift from God)..."** Biblical writers consistently recognized that God alone enjoys permanency and all creation self-destructs apart from his gift of shared immortality.

In Biblical literature God frequently declares that he is a jealous God who wants his own way: **"You shall have no other Gods before me."** He evaluates creation based upon utilization for His purpose. Resurrection is God's sharing life everlasting as he deems appropriate. Apart from him, *"life ends with a sigh ...because we are but dust."*

> "I know not what the future hath
> Of marvel or surprise,
> Assured alone that life and death
> God's mercy underlies."
> —*John Greenleaf Whittier*

BEHAVIOR IS THE LANGUAGE OF FAITH!

Shared Kingdom
Luke 22:14-30

There is no miracle or magic in the upper room. The scene defines Jesus' life as the revelation of God's eternal kingdom on earth. The sacrament is the message. There is no need to dig deep for understanding. The kingdom of God was revealed to the twelve, not in a personal mystical experience, but in a common meal that focused upon the common good.

Jesus confirmed up front that suffering is an issue when the kingdom of God confronts conflicting powers. Victory consists of sharing and giving thanks for God's transforming presence. The apostle Paul later said to first century Christians, **"for now we see in a mirror dimly, but then we shall see face to face. Now I know only in part, then I will know fully, even as I have been fully known."** Faith is defined as we live and share that for which we daily give thanks.

Personal betrayal subtly emerged at the table where all were gathered for the common meal. Is there any wonder that questions were asked among the twelve as to, *"who would do this?"* Immediately, *"A dispute arose among them as to which one of them was to be regarded as the greatest."* Once again, Jesus refocused the group, **"Who is greater, the one who is at the table or the one who serves? ...I am among you as one who serves."**

Two thousand years later Christians kneel at the communion rail and share a sacred meal that becomes a prelude to service or a self-indulgent betrayal. The words of Jesus apply to us as it did to the disciples, *"You are those who stood by me in my trials, and I confer on you, just as my Father has conferred on me, a kingdom, so that you may eat and drink at my table in my kingdom..."*

"By thy birth and by thy tears, By thy human grief and fears,
By thy conflict in the hour Of the subtle tempter's power;
Savior, look with pitying eye, Savior help or I die."
—*Robert Grant*

Justice And Righteousness
Amos 5:18-25

W e are fortunate to have access to public worship that enables us to share religious feelings through words, symbols, actions, and music. Admittedly, it can be a benign routine obligation. On the other hand, it can be a valuable time of shared thoughts and feelings if we prepare ourselves for a communal rather than a personal experience.

Amos makes it clear that the ingredients for meaningful shared worship must have practical application in non-religious activities or life would be unnaturally divided into secular and religious. The message of faith is that God is interested in righteous relationships among those who call themselves his children. Equally essential is divine presence and purpose. Centuries later, Jesus taught the importance of balance between love of God and love of neighbor.

Follow with reverent steps the great example
Of him whose holy work was doing good;
So shall the wide earth seem our Father's temple,
Each loving life a psalm of gratitude.
—John Greenleaf Whittier

BEHAVIOR IS THE LANGUAGE OF FAITH!

The Mission
Luke 10:1-12

The nearness of God's Kingdom is confirmed where healing and wholeness are in process. Otherwise, the experience is incomplete and of limited value. Priceless relationships develop among people with common needs. Empathy establishes emotional, conversational, and joyful bonds that outsiders only partially understand. The communal nature of salvation (wholeness) renders nonsensical the popular word combination "personal salvation." Although frequently used in a Christian context, it doesn't exist in the Bible. Jesus' message is unalterably bifocal. So, why does this combination exist and why is it so overused?

Those who are "becoming whole" make a point of going outside of their group to identify others with the same condition for the purpose of sharing the healing process. The Kingdom of God is near when the healing process is shared. How it is received is not under the control of those giving witness. Though some listeners respond with denial and rejection, others would like the opportunity to hear and see.

"And thus, we pray in deed and word,
Thy kingdom come on earth, O Lord,
In work that gives effect to prayer,
Thy purpose for thy world we share."
—*Methodist Hymnal*

BEHAVIOR IS THE LANGUAGE OF FAITH!

Full Time
Matthew 25:1-13

The creation account in Genesis tells us that Adam and Eve enjoyed a natural fellowship with God. Disruption resulted from human betrayal of God's trust. This was followed by alienation and a profound sense of guilt.

Immediately, God took measures to forgive, and to restore a creative relationship of trust accompanied by assurance of Divine presence and a sense of his purpose. Jesus reinforced this when he taught us to pray *"Thy will be done on earth as it is in heaven..."* He makes it clear that God's influence is preferable to life we develop on our own.

The destructive influence of evil is a chronic human condition that can be minimized only by the continuous influence of God's enabling power to do good. Paul wrote to the faithful in Rome, *"So I find it to be a law that when I want to do good, evil lies close at hand... Who will rescue me from this body of sin and death? Thanks be to God through Jesus Christ our Lord."*

The parable of the Ten Bridesmaids in Matthew teaches us to be prepared so that the transformation from this life to the next will be natural. God awareness is necessary.

Throughout the changing scenes of life,
In trouble and in joy,
The praises of my God shall still
My heart and tongue employ.
—*Tate and Brady*

BEHAVIOR IS THE LANGUAGE OF FAITH!

Time For Judging
Revelation 11:15-19

Jesus frequently told his followers not to judge others. Concerning himself he said *"I come not to judge."* Revelation 11:15-19 identifies the future as time for judgment. This "time to come" will be appropriate for judgment because then **"the kingdom of the world has become the kingdom of our Lord."**

The Book of Revelation was written for Christians under severe persecution. The writer was reminding them that their difficulties were not unexpected because they were at cross purposes with the value and reward system of the *"kingdom of this world."* It is difficult to remain steadfast on a course when the reward system is futuristic. Justice, righteousness, and common good are not primary concerns in the *"kingdom of this world"* that is focused upon immediate personal gratification. Christians, past, present and future, are challenged to manage the values of the Kingdom of God *("Thy will be done on earth as it is in heaven")* in an unfriendly environment. The Apostle Paul taught that neither the "planter: nor the "waterer" are primary; only God makes things grow. We are fellow workers with God. You are God's farm, God's building. The community of faith is God's work-product in process.

Our storehouse of daily decisions is a significant indicator as to whether or not we are *"in the world, but not of the world."* However, our earthly performance evaluation methods should not be compared with judgment that is final. Judgment is the sole prerogative of God, Who defers the process until **"the kingdom of the world has become the kingdom of our Lord."**

Work shall be prayer, if all be wrought
As thou wouldst have it done;
And prayer, by thee inspired and taught,
Itself with work be done.
—*John Ellerton*

The Works Themselves
John 14:1-14

On behalf of all believers who are too shy to make the request, Phillip asked Jesus to **"show us the Father."** It was a "show us the meat" type request that people want answered before they buy a burger or make a lifetime commitment. Verify, before you buy, is common sense.

Jesus' response was similar to the response of a college professor when asked an unnecessary question by an inattentive student "Where have you been all semester?" The disciples repeatedly heard Jesus teach and observed how he related to the crowds. Their questions and comments consistently showed a breakdown in communication and a failure to make the connection between the words and deeds of Jesus and God's eternal purpose.

"The Word became flesh" to glorify the Creator *"for no one could perform the signs that you do unless God were with him."* In the same way, the works of the children are evidence of faith that honors their Father. The Creator blesses the faithful with the presence of his Spirit that empowers the believer to practice *"justice, kindness, and humility in the Creator's presence."* Works are not an admission ticket to God's eternal banquet. Rather, they reflect free admission acknowledged by people of faith who honor the life and teachings of the one who said, *"To have seen me is to have seen the Father."*

Work, for the night is coming,
Work, through the morning hours,
Work, while the dew is sparkling,
Work, 'mid springing flowers,
Work, when the day grows brighter,
Work, in the glowing sun,
Work, for the night is coming,
When man's work is done.
—*Anna L. Coghill*

Deeds Of Power
Luke 19:28-40

J esus successfully resisted temptations to use power for his own benefit. He taught his followers to pray, *"Thy kingdom come. Thy will be done on earth as it is in heaven."* Yet, he did not leave a set of detailed arrangements for personal and institutional implementation of the Kingdom of God on earth. He clearly prepared his followers to be joyful that a few committed people can have on the general population. He compared the Kingdom of God to a small mustard seed hidden in the soil that produces a powerful flavor. Also, he pointed out that the Kingdom of God is similar to a dash of sourdough starter that imperceptibly yields a large loaf of bread.

"The whole multitude of the disciples began to praise God joyfully with a loud voice for all the deeds of power that they had seen." Sadly, the multitudes reduced to a few when they learned that the expectation, power, and direction of God's Kingdom are focused toward **"justice, kindness, and humility before God."** Jesus was a humble servant before he was a resurrected Lord. *"A servant is not greater than his master."*

Problems will always torment us
because all important problems
are insoluble: that is why they are important.
The good comes from the continuing struggle
to try and solve them, not from the
vain hope of their solution.
—*Arthur M. Schlesinger, Jr.*

BEHAVIOR IS THE LANGUAGE OF FAITH!

Unforced
Psalm 18; John 11:1-15

Psalm Eighteen is King David's poetic expression of how he understood his victory over King Saul as a blessing from God. One cannot help avoiding David's self-righteous portrayal of his good qualities as being rewarded appropriately by God. People who are both prosperous and religious frequently view their state of affairs as earned benefit. The Bible chronicles multiple expressions of this attitude along with a word of caution that such an orientation is spiritual quicksand.

King David demonstrated the wisdom saying, *"Pride cometh before the fall,"* when he arranged for the death of one of his loyal soldiers in order to add the soldier's wife to the royal harem.

From Genesis to Revelation, God's established corrective countermeasures repeatedly made His disappointment known, and exacted some measure of punishment for destructive behavior. Yet, He continues to utilize flawed humanity to effect outcomes that *"reflect God's own heart."* When you own the company, you can do whatever you want to do without explaining.

Unlike King David *"in soft robes living in royal palaces,"* Jesus authenticates his relationship with God when those who are broken are made whole and the poor hear *"good news."* All who humbly exchange their situational self-righteousness for the gift of God's eternal righteousness are truly blessed and will be a blessing to others.

What we have felt and seen
With confidence we tell;
And publish to the sons of men
The signs infallible.
—*Charles Wesley*

143

"Why Do You Hide?"
Psalm 44

When victory or defeat in human conflict is attributed to God, the underlying assumption is that God exerted special influence over the outcome. This is the opinion of the Psalmist who takes for granted that it is God's will for the enemies of Israel to slaughter communities and take their homes and possessions. Therefore, he is puzzled by Israel's defeat and humiliation at the hands of its enemies. He concludes that the defeat is no accomplishment of the Israelite's enemies. Rather, it occurred because *"God hid"* as the battle raged. One wonders if the Psalmist's puzzlement might have been better addressed had he acknowledged that God chooses to *"hide His face"* when human conflict results from competing interests that lack consideration for sacred influence.

The plan of God, in this sequence, appears to let those who *"live by the sword, die by the sword."* Undeniably, *"there are wars and rumors of wars;"* and, though victories are not permanent, there is no end to the imaginative means employed by the mighty to attribute victory to God.

Thankfully, in the midst of power and destruction there inevitably appears someone near to God who proclaims that His eternal purpose is to establish justice and kindness in personal and public relationships, and to exhibit humility before Sacred Presence. God-fearing people cannot escape temporal conflicts, but they can, through God's abiding presence, strive to manage the unpleasantness without attributing the outcome to God's preferential treatment. Might it be that the Psalmist presented a clear picture of the arenas of war when he said, *"God hides"* until, as Jesus says, he offers reconciliation to those who recognize the need?

Be thou my Vision, O Lord of my heart;
Naught be all else to me, save that thou art,
Thou my best Thought, by day or by night,
Waking or sleeping, Thy presence my light.
—*Eleanor H. Hull*

Hypocrisy
Matthew 23:1-36

A common problem is how to manage personal desire for the common good. This persistent challenge permeates every social structure. Our Bible lesson highlights the issue among religious professionals who routinely administer our storehouse of behavioral codes. Jesus valued their professional role and recommended that society do likewise. On the other hand, it is critical when public persona contradicts personal performance, as in "Strain a gnat and swallow a camel." Codes of conduct lend themselves to mechanistic administration imposed upon others but not upon those administrators who might be prone to act without conviction or commitment.

Hypocritical leadership encourages supporters to undervalue their performance on behalf of the common good. Codes of conduct exist to tutor individuals to serve the common good through implementation of justice and kindness in an attitude of humility before the Giver of Life. Although codes tutor, they have limited value apart from the primary guidance received from a sense of the presence of God. Human imperfection is a perpetual state of existence that requires guidance within and without. *"Woe to you, scribes and Pharisees, hypocrites! For you tithe mint, dill, and cumin, and have neglected the weightier matters of the law: justice and kindness and faith. It is these you ought to have practiced without neglecting the others."* God heals the imperfections of the repentant while permitting hypocrisy to self-destruct.

God, who touchest earth with beauty,
Make my heart anew;
With thy Spirit recreate me,
Pure and strong and true.
—*Mary S. Edgar*

Days To Come
Isaiah 2:1-5

The prophet speaks of *"days to come."* Like those of many great religious personalities, Isaiah's message constantly focused on the future. He suggested to his listeners that they live as citizens of the future because the present was seen as a hodgepodge of competing gods, each promoting a variety of values and diverse centers of worship.

Isaiah put together a religious description of the process of natural selection wherein the God of Jacob outlasts all other deities by *"teaching his ways"* and by *"judging and arbitrating"* conflicts so that people are able to live in peace. By human reckoning, God appears to be dragging out the enlightenment process to such an extent that we have to remind ourselves constantly that *"a thousand years in God's sight are but as yesterday when it is past, and as a watch in the night."* Numbers are useless when we attempt to fix a time when God began to bring order out of darkness and chaos. We are perceptive enough to realize that the creative effort is ongoing with every option that permits us to step into the light or step back into the darkness. Religion propagates both the greatest good and the greatest evil disseminated throughout the world. However, God utilizes everything that exists in an effort to enlighten us. The alternative to divine influence is a meaningless cycle of conflict and disorder. Isaiah points to the future and says, *"Come, let us walk in the light of the Lord."*

What tho' in solemn silence all
Move around the dark terrestrial ball?
What tho' no real voice nor sound
Amid the radiant orbs be found?
In reason's ear they all rejoice,
And utter forth a glorious voice;
Forever singing, as they shine,
"The hand that made us is divine."
—*Joseph Addison*

146

What Sort Of Man?
Matthew 8:18-27

Jesus was born a Jew and died a Jew. Yet, he redefined and reinterpreted thousands of years of Judaism as defined by Moses in light of the Ten Commandments and the Hebrew deliverance from slavery. The religious parameters of Judaism were unambiguous—God provides, believers obey, and everyone prospers. All of life's joys and sorrows were interpreted accordingly. Jesus offered a different interpretation wherein God is not exclusive, nor is He defined or bound by human categories, and His judgment is equated with neither adversity nor prosperity.

Jesus proclaimed passing of the old parameters of sin/guilt/judgment. He introduced the new creation by demonstrating control over the natural order before asking people to listen to his message of grace/forgiveness/gratitude influenced and empowered by God's abiding presence *"For the tree is known by the fruit it bears."*

Teach us, in every state,
To make thy will our own
And when the joys of sense depart,
To live by faith alone.
—*Augustus M. Toplady*

BEHAVIOR IS THE LANGUAGE OF FAITH!

147

Who Shall Ascend?
Psalm 24

The Psalmist asks the enduring question, *"Who shall ascend"* to the presence of God? This question arises in the thoughts of all who have a sense of Sacred Presence. Reasonably, those who have no such awareness have no need to ask the question. It is safe to say that a majority of people, past and present, primitive and modern, speak about Sacred Presence. Experiences and descriptions vary such that universal standards are not established. Into this maze, the Psalmist offers his observations and experiences.

He opens with a preconceived conviction that *"The earth is the Lord's and all that is within it."* Sacred Presence filters through thought and emotion as the indestructible origin of things that begin and end. Awareness is not the same as comprehension. Therefore, those who desire a more meaningful relationship must build upon initial awareness by doing what the Psalmist picturesquely refers to as *"ascend the hill of the Lord...and stand in his holy place."*

Three characteristics are important prerequisites for those who desire a more intense experience of Sacred Presence. First is to do what is right. **("clean hands.")** Second is to desire Sacred Presence **(*"pure heart."*)** Third is to refrain from misrepresenting one's self, **(*"do not swear deceitfully."*)** Cultivating these characteristics, one will *"receive blessing from God."* Clearly, Sacred Presence is inseparable from the way one lives because, *"The earth is the Lord's and all that is within it."* These three entry requirements are beyond human accomplishment. They serve their purpose when they encourage humility before God that receives a blessing rather than an arrogant attempt to be worthy of a blessing.

God's blessing is followed by *"vindication"* because the need for a more intimate sense of Sacred Presence implies neglect that produces remoteness. God acknowledges those who genuinely need a more intimate sense of Sacred Presence that affects desires, deeds, and self-understanding.

"Thou hidden Love of God, whose height,
Whose depth unfathomed, no man knows:
I see from far Thy beauteous light,
And only sigh for thy repose;
My heart is pained, nor can it be
At rest till it finds rest in Thee."
—*Gerhard Tersteegen*

BEHAVIOR IS THE LANGUAGE OF FAITH!

Wait For The Promise
Luke 1:1-11

The Bible assumes that all life emanates from God and moves progressively toward fulfillment that acknowledges His creative control. Prior to the anticipated *"fullness of time,"* humanity displays progress, or lack of progress, in fulfilling God's purpose. Impatiently, humans typically attempt to develop alternate plans of shorter duration with results that can be measured and universally understood.

As a practical matter, humans tend to focus upon the shorter plan that satisfies immediate needs and desires rather than upon God's long-term plan that progresses toward future fulfillment and gratification. In God's plan, believers are called upon to patiently and faithfully *"wait upon the Lord"* and *"wait for the promise."*

The appeal of God's plan is that it provides creative opportunities and an openness to change that serve His progressive purpose. In contrast, the human alternative might be compared to limited opportunity provided by an art kit

149

designed for painting by the numbers without concern for personal expression and development. Jesus pointed to the future when he told his followers, *"The one who believes in me will also do the works that I do and, in fact, will do greater works than these, because I am going to the Father."* God's plan requires that we prepare our thoughts, feelings, and behavior to *"receive the Spirit"* of change and do great things for the common good.

Standing on the promises that cannot fail,
When the howling storms of doubt and fear assail,
By the living Word of God I shall prevail,
Standing on the promises of God.
—*R. Kelso Carter*

Proper
Matthew 3

The public introduction of Jesus made it clear that he is one of us. Along with many others, he presented himself to John the Baptizer for baptism of repentance. The Baptizer hesitated to perform the rite because he considered Jesus too good to submit to public confession and cleansing. However, Jesus refused to distinguish himself from the flawed descendants of Adam and Eve. He repented as a human being for the sins of humanity. He was neither an outsider nor a hybrid.

The baptism of Jesus marked the beginning of the new creation. This is the basis for the Apostle Paul's referring to him as *"the second Adam."* Like a poor carpenter who builds with bent nails and crooked boards,

Jesus constructs his new creation with renovated social and religious rejects. *"And a voice came from heaven saying, 'This is my Son the Beloved, with whom I am well pleased'."*

> Jesus the sinner's friend, to thee,
> Lost and undone, for aid I flee,
> Weary of earth, myself, and sin,
> Open thine arms, and take me in.
> —*Charles Wesley*

BEHAVIOR IS THE LANGUAGE OF FAITH!

Gospel Of Hope
Colossians 1:1-23

C hristianity is a religion of hope not to be confused with wishful thinking or fantasy. Christian hope is result-oriented. Life that once was rebelliously estranged from the Creator enters a new relationship that advocates peace and does good things.

The motivation for holy living is based upon hope because the desired changes are a work in progress and not an accomplishment that qualifies boasting. Isaiah said that all of his righteousness is like a filthy rag in the presence of God. The desires that control us must be reoriented and self-gratification managed for a superior purpose. We turn to the Power that created life and humbly beg that we receive the will and strength to initiate and sustain the changeover.

We do not despair because progress is tediously slow. Jesus forewarned us that no matter where we are, evil is close at hand to reclaim and use us. He promised that God's presence and strength will be with us as it was with him. We have interesting and challenging decisions to make. We know what we are, but it is less clear what we will be.

Have Thine own way, Lord! Have Thine own way!
Thou art the potter, I am the clay.
Mold me and make me after Thy will,
While I am waiting, yielded and still.
—*Adelaide A. Pollard*

Judge Not
Luke 6:37-42

Jesus did not judge and neither should his followers. He was emphatic that judgment belongs to God who alone is just. Jesus utilized his time revealing God's redeeming and transforming presence. God is just and merciful and his judgment is final. Jesus was content with this arrangement and he moved on to proclaim and demonstrate the new beginning, not the end. He expected others to follow his lead. The Apostle Paul wrote to the community of faith in Philippi about the importance of maintaining a positive attitude toward potential—*"Not that I have already obtained this or have already reached the goal; but I press on to make it my own, because Christ Jesus has made me his own."* In matters of judgment, Jesus was unambiguous when pointing out that everyone has an impaired will. No one can properly pass judgment on the same condition in others. Jesus said, *"Do not judge, so that you may not be judged. For with the judgment you make you will be judged, and the measure you give will be the measure you get."* (Matthew 7:1-2)

Discomforting!

Social, political, and religious institutions have always addressed worldly consequences for intolerably destructive behavior. This is not the intended focus of God's redemptive community that is instructed by the Son, and empowered by the Spirit, to proclaim and promote change while leaving judgment to God. This does not suggest that we are unable to recognize and evaluate evil and destructive behavior on earth. God, who alone is righteous and knows all things, renders eternal judgment that is just.

Other refuge have I none,
Hangs my helpless soul on Thee;
Leave, ah! leave me not alone
Still support and comfort me.
All my trust on thee is stayed,
All my help from thee I bring;
Cover my defenseless head
With the shadow of thy wing.
—*Charles Wesley*

A New Thing
Isaiah 43:1-21

God said, *"You are mine... All are precious in my sight."* Isaiah was aware of this about five hundred fifty years before the birth of Christ. It was, and is, important for people *"passing through trials and tribulations"* to know and feel they belong to God and that they cannot be defined or defeated by adversity. **"Mine"** and **"My sight"** are key words because they reaffirm the basis for human relationship with God Who creates and redeems *"for His glory."*

Isaiah urges, *"Listen, everyone who is called by my name, whom I created for my glory, whom I formed and made... I am God, I am he... I work... You are my witnesses, says the Lord."* Much later, Jesus went to great lengths to make it clear **"I glorify the Father."**

"Do not remember the former things or consider the things of old. I am about to do a new thing." God is the one who put the old and the new deal together for all who need it. Acceptance means identifying with God's meaning and purpose that is learned and appreciated by paying attention. *"Thy will be done"* progressively replaces "I want" as sacred purpose influences behavior. Conviction enables one to say, with others of faith, *"Nothing can separate us from the love of God..."*

Discouraged in the work of life,
Disheartened by its load,
Shamed by its failures or its fears,
I sink beside the road.
But let me only think of Thee
And then new heart springs up in me.
—*Samuel Longfellow*

154

A Signal
Isaiah 11:1-10

Scripture represents God as one who consistently uses signals to attract attention without coercing a response. The Prophet Isaiah signals God's eternal purpose, and he suggests the proper path to fulfill that purpose.

First, Sacred Presence alone provides wisdom and understanding. Second, seekers are obligated to remain humble before God. These are necessary to accept the judgments of God as just in that they are not always based upon things seen and heard. The words and deeds of Jesus later reflected Isaiah's message concerning God's presence and purpose. Is there any doubt why the New Testament harkens back to Isaiah when validating the life of Jesus?

The signals provided by Isaiah and Jesus have generated countless words of interpretation and analysis down through the ages, but nothing has surpassed the rudimentary arrangement of the originals. The directions are clear if travelers keep the signals in sight.

> Brightly beams our Father's mercy
> From His lighthouse evermore,
> But to us He gives the keeping
> Of the lights along the shore.
> Let the lower lights be burning!
> Send a gleam across the wave!
> Some poor struggling, sinking sailor
> You may rescue, you may save.
> —*Philip P. Bliss*

BEHAVIOR IS THE LANGUAGE OF FAITH!

Summoned
Exodus 19:16-24

T he primitive worldview in the Bible presents creation as surrounded by water that is held back by a dome above and a dome below. All natural life existed within this sphere. Although our scientific worldview is different, cause and effect remains limited to arranging and rearranging people and objects within the sphere.

Religious people believe that the only exception to this dynamic is motivated by a universal mystical presence, variously named, that unmistakably attracts attention by effecting change. Every culture has a word for divinity. There are a few who view religion as a universal fantasy.

The Exodus text presents a distinctive event wherein God summoned Moses to receive tutorial commandments designed to enhance creative living that is consistent with divine meaning and purpose. Moses is pictured receiving the commandments alone on a high mountain covered in clouds that hid the face of God. As dramatic as it was, the Ten Commandments, and the hundreds of derivatives listed throughout the Old Testament, have not produced the desired results.

In contrast to Moses, the gospels tell us that God moved down from the mountain venerated by the birth of Jesus in a stable. Because words alone are limited by the boundaries of the "dome above and the dome below," Jesus walked the dusty dirty roads of Galilee where, in word and deed, he condensed the Ten Commandments and the six hundred ten derivatives to, *"Love God with all your mind, heart, soul, and strength and your neighbor as yourself."* He then said, *"to have seen me is to have seen the Father."*

I know not how that Bethlehem's babe
Could in the Godhead be;
I only know the manger child
Has brought God's life to me.
—*Harry Webb Farrington*
156

Prepare The Way

Luke 1:5-25; 57-80

The Bible consistently makes the point that God prepares the way for all that He does. Equally important is that His message is comprehensible to those for whom it is intended. Ordinary situations are used in extraordinary ways to communicate simple, but profound, messages that are durable.

God's preparation usually starts out with small factions not with the masses. One might say that God originated the 20/80 rule that says twenty percent of a group produces eighty percent of the results, while eighty percent are credited with the remaining twenty percent. Jesus made the observation that *"broad is the way that leads to destruction...and narrow is the way that leads to eternal life."* He also taught that it is God's will to have one hundred percent participation. He *"does not desire that one of his children should be lost."*

God follows through with preparation, guidance, and inspiration for those who welcome His influence to become involved effectively in proclaiming repentance, forgiveness, and transformation.

If thou but suffer God to guide thee,
And hope in Him through all thy ways,
He'll give thee strength, whate'er betide thee,
And bear thee through the evil days.
Who trusts in God's unchanging love
Builds on the rock that naught can move.
—*George Newmark*

BEHAVIOR IS THE LANGUAGE OF FAITH!

With You Always
Matthew 4:1-11; 28:18-20

In the beginning, Adam and Eve were tested. At the new beginning, Jesus was tested. The message is clear. No one places out of testing. Adding to the problem, the point of greatest vulnerability is the exact stress point upon which the greatest pressure is applied.

Adam and Eve are portrayed as desirous of knowledge like God's. They yielded to the temptation of disobedience to God's specific instructions. The Tester made good on his promise, and Adam and Eve experienced divine awareness of good and evil. The New Testament says that Jesus was tested after he was hungry, thirsty and alone in the wilderness for forty days. The Tester suggested that Jesus use his unique relationship with God to miraculously provide himself with food and water. Jesus rejected the suggestion that miracles are for personal advantage. They are to honor God who miraculously created all things.

The Tempter shifted to religion as an area to exploit human vulnerability. The suggestion was made that Jesus put his privileged relationship with God on public display by forcing God to intervene to save his life. Jesus refused to test God's love in order to prove a point. Finally, the Tempter offered to joint venture with Jesus to rule the universe. Jesus again declined and deferred to God as the sole creative power.

Jesus left the wilderness and devoted his life to serving God and seeking the common good for humanity. The Bible is unrelenting in making the point that good and evil are engaged in a joint venture for human development. Good is creative and is destined to be eternally victorious. Evil is self-destructive and, like a savage virus, forever dies with its final host. Jesus' final words as he sent his followers to a life of temptation and testimony *"I will be with you always."*

BEHAVIOR IS THE LANGUAGE OF FAITH!

Comfort
Isaiah 40:1-11

W ho among us needs *"comfort and a tender voice?"*; those who dwell in the desert of intense guilt and rejection or wander through life without meaning and purpose. Isaiah is God's messenger who announces there that is an escape route through the wilderness of spiritual, emotional, and physical highs and lows. Regardless of the route taken, those who receive benefit should know that it originates with God who provides continuity while constructing the only highway of deliverance that *"will stand forever."*

Isaiah reminded people that a shepherd's natural daily habit is to feed his flock and gently gather lambs to his bosom as he takes them to their mothers. A shepherd has one flock for which he is responsible. His way of being a good shepherd becomes for him the best way, not necessarily the most understood. God is the shepherd who responds to fundamental human need as described in Ecclesiastes 1:13, *"It is an unhappy business that God has given to human beings to be busy with."* Jesus identified himself as the permanent shepherd who is recognized and received by those who need what he offers.

Lord, it belongs not to my care
Whether I die or live;
To love and serve thee is my share,
And this thy grace must give.
—*Richard Baxter*

BEHAVIOR IS THE LANGUAGE OF FAITH!

Blasphemy
Mark 3:20-30

As a practical matter, we accept our compulsory participation in the conflict between good and evil. There is no "time out," and there is no other game in town. The pre-scientific culture in which Jesus was reared did not understand natural phenomena based upon scientific cause-and-effect analysis. They perceived adversity as punishment for evil deeds.

When Jesus healed illness, it demonstrated the power of good defeating evil in the afflicted person. These acts were episodic. There are no reports of mass healings. The primary purpose of the demonstrations was that Jesus' authority came from God. Those who opposed Jesus did not deny the occasions of healing; however, they branded them as deceptive works of the evil one.

Jesus used this event to enlighten people that the purpose of creative healing is to overcome destructive evil. Since the powers of good and evil are beyond the understanding and control of humanity, Jesus publicly associated his healing with total reliance upon the creative power of God. Conflict between good and evil remain. It is beneficial to perpetually prepare mind and emotion to recognize evil and take counter-measures by participating actively in good that overcomes evil.

Because of their religious specialization, the Pharisees were less prone to adopt the nonconforming methods of Jesus as he revealed the transforming power of God's goodness. Jesus warned them that misidentifying good as evil results from being so self-possessed that the creative characteristics of good become difficult to recognize.

Thou art the truth, thy Word alone true wisdom can impart;
thou only canst inform the mind and purify the heart.
—George W. Doane

Kindred Spirit
Mark 3:31-33

F amily relationships are important in Biblical literature. The Ten Commandments include honoring father and mother. Responsibilities for distressed family members are detailed in Leviticus. Matthew opens with a detailed genealogy of Jesus' ancestry to connect him with the promises God made to his forbearers. In light of this, it is especially significant that Matthew reported an episode where Jesus snubbed his family members wanting to see him and explained it by saying, *"Whoever does the will of God is my brother, and sister, and mother."*

Behavior that reflects God's creative and redemptive purpose is a more binding basis for relationships than genetic identity, no matter how tender. In another context Jesus makes the same point when he says: *"He who loves father or mother more than me is not worthy of me; and he who loves son or daughter more than me is not worthy of me; and he who does not take up his cross and follow me is not worthy of me. He who finds his life will lose it, and he who lose his life for my sake will find it."* (Matthew 10:37-39)

These emotional words established the priority of God's creative purpose revealed in the flesh through Jesus.

> Blest be the tie that binds
> Our hearts in Christian love
> The fellowship of kindred minds
> Is like to that above.
> —John Fawcett

BEHAVIOR IS THE LANGUAGE OF FAITH!

161

Keep Awake
Mark 13:1-13; 24-37

Jesus was an accommodating person who used every available means to help people connect with the Life-Giver. Although Temple worship had its limitations, it was a community institution that influenced behavior. Jesus worshiped and taught in the Temple, but he never elevated it beyond the status of a temporary community center for religious purposes.

When Jesus told the disciples that the day would come when the Temple with its immensity and majesty would be destroyed, they wanted a "heads up" as to when. Jesus gave no timetable. He told them that natural events with which they were familiar would continue to occur and should be considered as the beginning of birth pangs that precede new life.

The community of believers is responsible for proclaiming the *"good news"* to all the world, knowing that the Spirit influences their thoughts and words as best suits the situation. With regard to the end of creation, God alone knows the details as He alone knows the details of the beginning. Jesus' advice is to *"keep awake"* until the *"Son of Man...with great power and glory...gathers his elect."*

When I shall reach that happy place, I'll be forever blest,
For I shall see my Father's face, And in His bosom rest.
Filled with delight my raptured soul
Lives out its earthly day;
And then, though Jordan's waves may roll,
I'll fearless launch away.
—*Samuel Stennett*

Stand Up
Luke 21:25-36

The New Testament teaches that Jesus, in a temporary limited setting, revealed the creative power and glory of God. Jesus shared his arena with the destructive power of evil. This arrangement will endure until the end of time. Neutrality is a fantasy that is not identified or described in the Bible through fact, myth, or metaphor.

Destructive power is not eternal. Rather, this parasitic prevaricator is mysteriously an advocate of God that exists to test the human spirit created to "overcome evil with good." Jesus described the test as a choice between life and death. The seriousness of the matter is sufficient for believers to **"Be on guard so that your hearts are not weighed down in dissipation...and that day does not catch you unexpectedly..."**

To aid humanity in making decisions, God provides tutorial laws designed to prepare the way for a receptive response to the life and teachings of Jesus. He revealed the limits of legalism and elevated sacred relationship above codification. Commandments alone are susceptible to human manipulation. Religious codes facilitate the convenient, but erroneous, perception that life can be separated into sacred and secular categories. Jesus scrambles sacred and secular into a unified ingredient for a single purpose that he describes in this prayer:

"That they may all be one. Just as you,
Father, are in me and I am in you,
may they also be in us,
so that the world may believe
that you have sent me." John 17:21

BEHAVIOR IS THE LANGUAGE OF FAITH!

The Plan
Psalm 146

The Psalmist was attempting to touch people for whom life was not pleasant; powerful oppressors controlled their lives through a system of cultural injustice. Typically, vulnerable people suffer because the attitudes and actions of those in control are unaffected by a sense of Sacred Presence that motivates an interest in the common good.

His message was one of hope to the oppressed who lived according to the whims of their oppressors. He assured them that selfish devices of mortals are limited and temporary. They must not despair because the time will come when the oppressors will be replaced by others who implement just and righteous behavior.

This is not an easy message to deliver or an easy one to receive by those who want and need immediate relief. The Psalmist expressed unconditional trust in God's timeless plan wherein justice and righteousness evolve to serve the common good and honor the Creator. *"The Lord will reign forever,"* and good shall exist after time and testing sift out impurities. Critics of this message say that it encourages people to submit to oppression and find gratification in looking for an idyllic future provided by God to those who believe in the promise. However, this is a misperception of the Biblical message that focuses upon God's *"...will be done on earth as it is in heaven."*

"In holy contemplation, We sweetly then pursue
The theme of God's salvation, and find it ever new.
Set free from present sorrow we cheerfully can say,
E'en the unknown tomorrow bring with it what it may."
—*William Cowper*

"The Time Is Near"
Revelation 1:1-8

The Revelation account was written during a time of intense persecution of Christians by the Emperor of Rome. Thousands of Christians were killed because their teachings were strange and foreign to the Roman culture. As a practical matter, Roman government was tolerant of all religions unless they challenged Roman authority. Christians teaching that Jesus was Lord and King gave the Emperor a basis for identifying them as enemies of the state as well as the ones responsible for other current problems in Rome.

The author of Revelation forewarned the community of faith that the evil powers of the day would bring suffering and death upon them and that they would be powerless to effectively resist. John's message is timeless because *"the time is near"* and believers always need to remain prepared. Jesus taught the same message that no one knows when the end will come for individuals or for the universe. However, individually it is never far away. The prudent thing is to always live with gratitude by enhancing the quality of life that is given. Time is a synthetic tool that measures the length of God's investment. We can only imagine eternity as God's gift to those who feel secure through a sustained openness to His presence.

"Be still, my soul: thy God doth undertake
To guide the future, as He has the past.
Thy hope, thy confidence let nothing shake;
All now mysterious shall be bright at last.
Be still, my soul: the waves and winds still know
His voice Who ruled them while He dwelt below."
—*Katharina Von Schlegel*

BEHAVIOR IS THE LANGUAGE OF FAITH!

165

Cycle Of Grace
Matthew 18:21-35

"**O**vercoming evil by doing good" is a lifelong behavioral modification program. It requires change from our natural inclination toward self-gratification to concern for the common good. God's grace prevents ultimate failure for those who continually develop new ways of thinking and behaving that reflect God's creative influence. The primary criteria for evaluating progress centers upon what is done that glorifies God. Verbal affirmation of creeds and doctrines cannot be used as substitutes.

The parable in Matthew teaches us how deeply ingrained is our sense of self-importance. To this mindset, Jesus brings a message of God's forgiving and redeeming love that unchains us from a determined past and frees us to be forgiving and redeeming in our relationships with others. Yet our natural thoughts and feelings insist upon drawing us back toward a personal religion that filters all that we think and do through a funnel of personal salvation. Although the sentiment is warm and fuzzy, it is not Christian to think of ourselves as exceptional among God's children. Jesus said, *"Even as you have done it unto the least of these my brethren, you have done it unto me."* The gospel makes it clear that, **"God so loved the world..."**

Equality exists on earth only with regard to the fact of birth and death. Otherwise, life is not fair, just, or righteous. The gift of life provides each generation the opportunity for a joint venture between God and humanity to cultivate *"justice and kindness"* in interpersonal relationships, while maintaining a state of *"humility in the presence of God."* God alone evaluates performance and measures progress. The community of faith is called upon to witness in word and deed His divine presence and power.

Come, let us, who in Christ believe,
Our common Savior praise,
To Him with joyful voices give
The glory of His grace.
—*Charles Wesley*

Wisdom And Power
Ecclesiastes 9:13-18

The desire for wisdom needs cultivation. The desire for power needs control. Wisdom and power should not be viewed as compatible. They are not naturally bound however, society benefits when they work in unison. The prevailing matchup unites power and tyranny with disastrous social consequences.

The masses obviously find it difficult to learn that people elevated to positions of power customarily do not work for the well-being of the powerless. The powerful typically consider themselves naturally superior and deserving of their position of control over "lesser folks." Too frequently the powerless share this view of their inferiority and routinely acquiesce to the control of others.

The writer of Ecclesiastes provides us with a timeless lesson when he contrasts the benefits derived from a poor man's wisdom that was quickly forgotten and derided in deference to the *"shouting of a ruler among fools."* Jesus taught that those who are meek in God's presence will never have power and control on earth because their values come from divine inheritance. *"See, I am sending you out like sheep into the midst of wolves; so be wise as serpents and innocent as doves."* (Matthew 10:16)

The things unknown to feeble sense,
Unseen by reason's glimmering ray,
With strong commanding evidence
Their heavenly origin display.
—Charles Wesley

BEHAVIOR IS THE LANGUAGE OF FAITH!

God With Us
Matthew 1:18-25

There have always been devoted Christians who stumble intellectually over the virgin birth account reported in Matthew and Luke. The simple message is that Jesus is *"God with us."* The creation account in the opening chapters of Genesis and the virgin birth account are not in the measured language of science.

The creation of Adam from dust and the virgin birth of Jesus portray a Sacred Immortal Presence that manipulates all matter according to divine purpose. The Bible attributes human predisposition to sin as the result of propagation from Adam to all of his descendants in a similar way that an infected male propagates aids in his children.

Jesus was spared contamination because a sinful male did not impregnate Mary. The second Adam of the new creation was conceived by the sacred power of the Creator. Words cannot define or measure God. Therefore, science has no mechanism for addressing transactions involving the sacred and the profane.

The first creation account involving Adam and the new creation account involving Jesus convey the same message that *"God is with us."* The sin of Adam provides insight into human self-centeredness. The life, death, and resurrection of Jesus provide insight into the redemptive and transforming power of Sacred Presence (God with us). The accounts are validated by results. Disembodied words are meaningless babble. The lifelong challenge to all who have a sense of Sacred Presence is to overcome evil (Adam's heritage) by doing good (Jesus' enlightenment).

God of the past, our times are in thy hand;
With us abide.
Lead us by faith to hopes true promised land;
Be thou our guide.
With thee to bless, the darkness shines as light,
And faith's fair vision changes into sight.
—*Hugh T. Kerr*

Renewal
Isaiah 40:1-11; 28-31

What happens when evil prevails and humans succumb to temptation resulting in destruction and guilt? Some experience a deeply-felt need for relief. Others feel no burden or need for comfort.

Those among us who claim to be spiritually connected tend to assume erroneously that everyone is aware of a spiritual dimension. The prophet says that those who experience the need for comfort receive it from God who is attentive to the *"least and the lost."*

One aspect of spirituality is an overwhelming feeling of guilt that follows decisions with destructive consequences. As intense heat from the sun makes a flower fade, so guilt diminishes the bloom and beauty of an otherwise creative and productive life. What makes the situation very difficult to manage is persistent temptation that encourages repetition. Temptation that leads to destructive behavior is not limited to a single event. Rather, it provides a level of gratification that intensifies the desire to repeat. Such power and influence is too often greater than one can resist. Guilt alerts us to danger but provides no solution.

Isaiah tells those who recognize that they are entrapped that God is the only being powerful enough to intervene *("if you are my servant...")* and interrupt the cycle of destructive routine and guilt. Where sorrow and sadness cry out, God provides comfort and renewal for *"the least and the lost..."*

Guilt, like pain, can serve as a warning that something needs to be done differently. Release from a guilt-laden past and renewal for the present is God's plan to overcome evil by doing good.

O what a blessed hope is ours!
While here on earth we stay,
We more than taste the heavenly powers,
And antedate that day:
We feel the resurrection near,

169

Our life in Christ concealed,
And with his glorious presence here
Our earthen vessels filled.
—*Charles Wesley*

Show Me
Psalm 86

Trust in a good, forgiving, and loving God is the timeless foundation of the Bible's redemptive message. This portrait is beautifully framed by those who genuinely feel the need for redemption. Otherwise, there is no perceived reason for a God who is patient, merciful, gracious, faithful, and loving.

The Psalmist pleads with God to *"show me a sign of your favor."* People in need desperately long for assurance that help is coming. Correct diagnosis might rivet a person's attention, but it's the remedy that engages the whole body in grateful response. Generations later, Jesus extended an offer, saying, *"Come unto me all who labor and are heavy laden and I will give you rest."* Those who are unmindful of deity should not be held in contempt simply because they suffer no need for God's patience, mercy, graciousness, faithfulness, and love.

In the case of the Psalmist, the perceived need was victory over the enemies of Israel. The help and comfort he wanted was a defeated enemy. Centuries later, Jesus did not minimize basic physical need for food, clothing, shelter, and secure surroundings. However, he was emphatic that the satisfaction of physical needs might not result in contentment. He prioritized by saying, *"Seek first the kingdom of God and his righteousness and all these things will be given (put in proper perspective) to you as well."* Church history is filled with people who voluntarily deprived themselves of physical needs in order to remain focused upon their relationship with God. A sense of dependence upon God is a human characteristic

170

that is commonly demonstrated in work, war, and worship. Like the composer of the Eighty-sixth Psalm,

"In the day of my trouble I call on you,
for you answer me...
For you are great and do wondrous things;
you alone are God.
Teach me your way, O Lord,
that I may walk in your truth,
give me an undivided heart
to revere your name."

Darkness To Light
Isaiah 9:1-11

Isaiah's message of divine deliverance was particularly meaningful to his audience because they had lived under the domination of a foreign king for a long time. Predictions of a better time provided hope that enhanced a positive attitude in the oppressed. However, hope dims and disappointment becomes despair when they are based upon assurances from those who exude authority without actually having any.

How does one distinguish authentic sources of hope from those who merely gratify wishful thinking? Isaiah offers four words as tools for authentication.

• The first is **WISDOM.** As used in the Bible, it is the quality attributed to God reflected in the orderly creation and maintenance of heaven and earth. When applied to a person, it refers to creative living that exemplifies balance between reason and faith. A wise person seeks to avoid Adam's and Eve's mistake of seeking knowledge so *"they would be like God, knowing good and evil."* Wisdom manages knowledge.

171

- The second validation is that wisdom is an advocate of **PEACE.** Conflict is the norm among competing centers of power. The desire for power to control is often used by false authoritarians who fashion their message of hope in a way that makes personal servants of their followers.
- The third characteristic of wisdom is **JUSTICE** wherein people strive again and again to revise and manage human affairs in a fashion that fairly serves the many—not only the few.
- The fourth distinguishing characteristic is **RIGHTEOUSNESS** which is derived from a proper alignment with God in a Master-servant relationship. This is offered in the Lord's Prayer *"Thy Kingdom come, thy will be done on earth as it is in heaven."* One Master is a righteous arrangement. Jesus prayed, *"Not my will but thine be done."*

His wisdom ever waketh,
His sight is never dim;
He knows the way he taketh,
And I will walk with him.
—*Anna L. Waring*

I And The Children
Hebrews 2:10-18

In Genesis we read where God's first children ate of the **"Tree of Knowledge"** for the purpose of knowing things as God knows. God was alarmed by this and immediately put protection around the **"Tree of Life"** to prevent Adam and Eve from living forever with new-found knowledge that they were incapable of managing for the highest and best use. Knowledge of good and evil continues to be available to all of Adam's and Eve's descendants.

The subject of eternal life from which Adam, Eve, and their descendants are constrained involves a much broader context than knowledge—so broad that the word "personal" has limited application. The term "personal salvation" is so restrictive that it borders upon being an oxymoron. It is used appropriately as a prerequisite to community well-being about which Jesus is quoted as saying, *"Here am I and the children God has given me."*

Rebirth is a joint venture involving all who receive from God the gift of a restored relationship that is eternal. Any suggestion that the gift is personally accessed and utilized, as one would acquire and use personal knowledge, is misdirected. We are born into a family of believers whom we join in a common cause that glorifies the Father who gives life. As is written about Jesus' communal connection, *"Since, therefore, the children share flesh and blood, he himself likewise shared the same things...he had to become like his brothers and sisters in every respect...because he himself was tested by what he suffered, he is able to help those who are being tested."*

Salvation is characterized by what is shared rather than by what personally is known.

"Teach us to utter living words
Of truth which all may hear,
The language all men understand
When love speaks loud and clear;
Till every age and race and clime
Shall blend their creeds in one,
And earth shall for one brotherhood
By whom thy will be done."
—*Henry H. Tweedy*

Out Of The Heart
John 7:37-39

Jesus made it plain that his crowd appeal was based upon need *("Let anyone who is thirsty come to me")* and willingness to receive what is given *("and let the one who believes in me drink")*. The word "ought" is not mentioned. Why should it be? Need does not require convincing or regulating because it originates from a sense of deprivation. The poetry of Isaiah tell us:

> *"In the path of your judgments, O Lord, we wait for you; your name and renown are the soul's desire. My soul yearns for you in the night, my spirit within me earnestly seeks you."*

Water and thirst are the topic of another important event where Jesus teaches that through him God addresses our deepest need. He told the Samaritan woman by the well:

> *"If you knew the gift of God, and who it is that is saying to you, 'Give me a drink,' you would have asked him, and he would have given you living water...The water that I give will become in them a spring of water gushing up into eternal life."*

There are degrees of need just as there are levels of thirst. Regardless, the common denominator is that satisfaction relates to need. Need satisfaction produces a reservoir that overflows

> *"...thou anointest my head with oil. My cup runneth over."*

Christian faith never remains private because it is based upon excess resulting from God's generosity. Capacity is constantly changing, and content is continually overflowing. Quantification and judgment are too complex and are

174

necessarily left to God's justice. Recipients are called upon to manage the overflow to the glory of God and the needs of others.

I need Thee every hour,
In joy or pain;
Come quickly and abide,
Or life is in vain.
—*Anne S. Hawks*

Adopted Heirs
Galatians 3:23-4:7

L aws that govern human conduct are necessary because unsupervised behavior can be intolerably destructive. Undisciplined desires can result in social chaos. Society more or less observes its laws to maintain order. Laws are also important in maintaining religious conformity. Religious laws differentiate between varieties of religions, each with its own set of particulars. The tutorial function of religious laws is to define appropriate behavior, determine guilt regarding disobedience, and establish consequences. The shortcoming of religious laws is the dilution of their tutorial value when they become absolute and generate resentment under the guidance of religious professionals who choose to use them to maintain established ecclesiastical structures.

Yet, the purpose of religion is to enhance personal and communal relationships with Sacred Presence who exercises more profound influence than is possible with codes of conduct.

Jesus was very upset that religious laws, enforced by physical consequences and guilt, were intolerable burdens on the general population. He offered an alternative message of forgiveness that lifted the burden of guilt. Paul, in Galatians, characterized followers of Jesus as children of God adopted through faith in his redeeming, forgiving, and transforming presence that could not be accomplished under the Law. The Law uses guilt as a means of exercising control. God's forgiving grace makes possible a creative relationship that affects behavior and serves the common good.

> Almighty God of truth and love,
> to me thy power impart;
> The mountain from my soul remove,
> the hardness from my heart.
> O may the least omission pain
> my reawakened soul,
> And drive me to that blood again,
> Which makes the wounded whole.
> —Charles Wesley

Assigned Field
II Corinthians 10:1-18

The *"meekness and gentleness of Christ"* describes the character of Christian good news proclaimed in an environment accustomed to conflict, power, and acquisition. Christians are called upon to rely upon this influence to confront *"arguments and proud obstacles"* against the *"knowledge of God."* The gospel is never forced or coerced upon others because it is designed to address the needs of those who hear it rather than to bolster the weak faith of some who proclaim it.

God's involvement is evidenced by activity that *"builds up"* rather than **"tears down."** I am reminded of two pre-school children in my grandmother's living room playing with building blocks they received during Christmas. One was very skilled and put together a very neat castle. The other was much less imaginative and was in such a hurry that his work repeatedly toppled over. The better builder left the room and returned with grandmother only to find that the frustrated child had knocked down the neat castle. Typically, frustrated children and adults express their inadequacy by tearing down what others cultivate and build. Sacred Presence inclines a willing heart to be creative in a way that serves the common good and honors the Creator—not the individual; this is called testimony.

Christian faith is about God's gift—not independent accomplishment. In prayer we address God as *"Father"* because He is the giver of life. We refer to Jesus as Savior because He is the redeemer of life. Therefore, as Christians, *"we keep within the field that God has assigned us,"* that is to give evidence of His creative and redeeming presence.

There is a balm in Gilead
to make the wounded whole;
There is a balm in Gilead
To heal the sin-sick soul.
If you can't preach like Peter,
If you can't pray like Paul,
Just tell the love of Jesus,
And say he died for all.
—*American Folk Hymn*

Entrusting The Message
II Corinthians 5:16-21

N agging discomfort results when there is separation from natural attachments such as exist between parent and child. The fundamental Biblical conviction is that humanity is separated from God in a similar way that is difficult to define. There is a relentless longing for relief and a persistent search for an example of someone who is connected. The example must be simple and unmistakable or we miss it.

Paul tells the Corinthian community of faith that Jesus is the example of life connected to Sacred Presence. This makes him the beginning of a new creation of connected people. The original connection between God and Adam resulted in separation and discomfort. Jesus proclaimed the message of reconciliation. Those who feel comfortable with the first creation feel no need for reconciliation offered by the second creation. Paul's letter is addressed to those who feel the need. His message proclaims God's love that enables reconciliation.

Those who feel connected are now entrusted with Jesus' message, and *"their trespasses are not counted against them."* The nearness of God in a reconciled life generates an appreciation for the passage in Philippians that *"whatever is true, whatever is honorable, whatever is just, whatever is pure, whatever is pleasing, whatever is commendable, if there is any excellence and if there is anything worthy of praise, think about these things."*

Thou grantest pardon through thy love;
Thy grace alone availeth.
Our works could ne'er our guilt remove;
Yea, e'en the best life faileth.
For none may boast himself of aught,
But must confess thy grace hath wrought
Whate'er in him is worthy.
—Martin Luther

Contrast
Ephesians 4:17-32

Paul reminds the Christian community in Ephesus that their conduct is very important because they are a minority living in a pagan land. Their lifestyle should present a sharp contrast to the prevailing lifestyle. The contrast is not for any self-serving purpose. Rather, it is intended to reflect the *"mark and seal"* of Sacred Presence that empowers change. It is similar to an athlete's saying that his style of play reflects his willingness to adapt to the way he is coached.

Absent the wisdom of God, people are left with behavior that is naturally self-serving and self-indulgent. Paul provides us with a clear understanding of how this plays out: *"bitterness and wrath and anger and wrangling and slander, together with all malice."* The wisdom of God motivates *"being kind to one another, forgiving one another, as God in Christ has forgiven you."*

Paul's point is that we cannot be host to the enemy and serve as effective participants in the unfolding divine plan to overcome the destructive consequences of evil. *"No one serves two masters."* The fact that the enemy too frequently breaks down our defenses and scores a victory is no reason to make it perpetually convenient. Be loyal and maintain the contrast.

"Though oft I seem to tread alone
Life's dreary waste, with thorns o'er grown,
The voice of love, in gentlest tone,
Still whispers, 'Cling to me!'"
—*Charlotte Elliott*

BEHAVIOR IS THE LANGUAGE OF FAITH!

Signs And Presence
John 3:1-8

Nicodemus was a very conscientious Jewish religious leader who was comfortable with his beliefs based upon the traditions of his ancestors. Yet, he was open to new religious experiences and concepts. Based upon his opening conversation with Jesus, he was amazed and puzzled by what Jesus said and did before the crowds. In terms of his personal experience, he was unable to evaluate and catalogue what he had seen and heard. What caused Nicodemus to have difficulty relating to Jesus?

What he saw and heard was different from anything he had previously experienced. He had no basis to process it, to know what purpose it served, or to comprehend how it related to the spiritual needs of the people for whom he was a rabbi. Nicodemus owed it to himself and his flock to determine the credibility of Jesus' teaching and the inexplicable signs that accompanied his message. He had a need to make sense of Jesus because there were other practitioners of magical things, some of whom exploited and misguided people.

Nicodemus questioned, but did not challenge, Jesus as to his identity and purpose. The signs Jesus performed displayed such control over the forces of nature and were so beneficial to others that Nicodemus felt they were obviously empowered by God. The crowds who heard Jesus teach and saw his signs were also great admirers.

All of us can relate to Nicodemus because we likewise have difficulty with the practicality of following what Jesus said and did. Jesus presented a new concept, a new heaven, and a new earth. It was difficult for Nicodemus to find an emotional home for this new way of life. It is also difficult for most people to do so. The directions Jesus gave to Nicodemus are equally applicable to us.

We must initiate a new beginning that relies upon God's knowledge of us rather than our knowledge of God. Nothing in human experience is more primitive than awareness of Sacred Presence. The life that Jesus displayed was *"born from above,"* and his credibility relied upon that sacred abiding presence's influencing what he said and did. We, like Nicodemus, are given the choice of a religion based upon knowledge that we can control or upon a sacred relationship to which we can relate. *"What is born of the flesh is flesh, and what is born of the Spirit is spirit."* Humility is the desire to conform to God's influence. Arrogance is the desire for God to conform to our influence.

Years ago I heard a story about the gold-rush days of the old west. An old gold-miner came down from the hills to a small town to buy supplies. It had been two months since he and his donkey had come to town; to say the least he appeared bedraggled. As they passed in front of the saloon a young cowboy staggered out of the saloon and called out to the old miner who ignored him. He called out again. By this time a couple of his buddies joined him from the saloon. He pulled his six-shooter and fired near the old man's feet saying "Old man, I want to see you dance." With that said, he began firing off more rounds near the old man's feet. The old man began to dance around after each shot. After emptying both six shooters, the cowboy turned toward the crowd laughing and waiving his pistols. Suddenly his buddies stopped laughing. The cowboy turned to see what was happening. The old miner had lifted his buffalo rifle from his donkey's pack and aimed it right between the cowboy's eyes. He said, "Son, have you ever kissed the rear-end of a donkey?" The cowboy replied, "No sir, but, I have always wanted to."

O for a faith that will not shrink,
Though pressed by every foe,
That will not tremble on the brink
Of any earthly woe!
—*William H. Bathurst*

BEHAVIOR IS THE LANGUAGE OF FAITH!

Authority
Numbers 27:12-23

Conditional authority is the Biblical norm for institutional religion. Religious leaders with varying degrees of authority and competence are practical necessities because people, like sheep, do not perform well without a shepherd. Religious authority must be filtered before it is bestowed. In the case of Joshua, the *"blessing"* by a former successful leader was important. In addition, his acceptance by other religious leaders, and the community, cleared his pathway to leadership.

Why is all of this layering necessary? The answer lies in the temptation of those in power to misdirect their effort. Leadership in a religious community is not about the leader. It is about the Creator and about finding the most effective way to manage the creation for His glory. Unfortunately, even with all of the checkpoints, religious leaders can drift from their calling and use the power and influence of their position to manipulate the community for self-serving purposes. The Bible goes out of the way to record both the successes and failures of those whom God has chosen to guide the spiritual development of others.

The Bible records the history of prominent religious leaders who, unlike Joshua, aligned themselves with the power of kings and other political officials for the purpose of exploitation. However, human inadequacy is incapable of marginalizing God's power and influence. Like-minded people find each other and find ways to legitimize their common interests for good or for evil. Joshua sought the common good when he stood before his friends and neighbors, with whom he had spent forty years in the wilderness, and said to them in their hour of decision: *"Now if you are unwilling to serve the Lord, choose this day whom you will serve...but as for me and my household, we will serve the Lord."*

Faith of our fathers, we will love
Both friend and foe in all our strife;
And preach thee too, as love knows how

By kindly words and virtuous life.
Faith of our fathers, holy faith!
We will be true to thee till death.
—*Frederick W. Faber*

Overwhelmed And Forgiven
Psalm 65

The Psalmist praises God Who answered His children's desperate prayers for rain in time of drought. Since they believed that prosperity was reward for good behavior and that natural disaster was God's response to disobedience, it was appropriate for them to blame their bad behavior for their hardship. The Psalmist expressed gratitude because God was willing to forgive their often-repeated self-destructive decisions of disobedience **("When deeds of iniquity overwhelm us, You forgive our transgressions...")** and addressed their needs. The world view of that day was uncomplicated in that destruction was a consequence of evil and prosperity was a consequence of good. All of life was understood in terms of either column "A" or column "B." Regardless of their world view, their experience and conviction was that when they were overwhelmed by destructive conditions, they found security in God's ability and willingness to respond to their situation when they expressed the proper attitude of contrition.

Time is precious to all living things. Therefore, we value the short version of cause and effect and we wish God would handle things in a timely manner rather than take eons to make his point. Since we do not control the time frame, we are able to share our limited experience over the centuries and cultures. Evidence indicates that over time it is advantageous for people to value and seek the Sacred Presence of the universe and manage affairs in a manner that is compatible. Much religious activity is arrogantly focused upon knowing and understanding God. A more effective effort should be based upon the comforting realization that God knows us and patiently awaits our willingness to allow his influence in the management of our daily affairs *("Be still and know that I am God! I am exalted among the nations, I am exalted in the earth.")*

One of the greatest challenges to spiritual growth is expressed in Psalm 119:15, *"I will meditate on your precepts and fix my eyes on your ways."* Sharing religious knowledge and experience with others provides valuable social underpinning for our beliefs.

> Ever present, truest friend,
> ever near thine aid to lend,
> Leave us not to doubt and fear,
> groping on in darkness drear:
> When the storms are raging sore,
> hearts grow faint and hopes give o'er.
> Whispering softly, Wanderer, come.
> Follow me, I'll guide thee home.
> —*Marcus M. Wells*

BEHAVIOR IS THE LANGUAGE OF FAITH!

Asking And Listening
Luke 2:41-52

This is the only childhood event in the life of Jesus that Luke chose to put in his historical account. Twelve-year-old Jesus, in the Temple, listening and asking question of learned religious leaders, was clearly intended to show his

184

involvement with institutional religion from the beginning. He was receptive to what experienced people had to say about religious affairs. His questions astounded the elders. His religious family life is implied by their presence in Jerusalem for a religious celebration.

Luke wants us to realize that the nurture of friends and family, along with institutional religion, gave Jesus intellectual and emotional underpinning for what was ahead of him. Luke's point is unmistakable that early childhood religious development was an essential part of God's plan and purpose for Jesus' life.

Religion can be so badly mismanaged that it destroys the very purpose for which it exists. Jesus came teaching and healing to demonstrate God's transforming presence and power in his life. The people in the street marveled at the things he did. However, institutional religion and politics condemned him to die. Ironically, as a child he listened, learned, and embodied all that the institution taught him. As an adult the institution rejected him. Jesus never abandoned his institutional ties because he understood that, flawed as it is, institutional religion is important for spiritual development. For this reason, he prayed upon the cross, ***"Father, forgive them, for they know not what they do."***

Religion is the personal and communal response to Sacred Presence. This is the way the Creator designed the system. We prayerfully and meditatively seek His guidance as to how best it can be done.

> Mid toil and tribulation,
> And tumult of her war,
> She waits the consummation
> Of peace forevermore;
> Till, with the vision glorious,
> Her longing eyes are blest,
> And the great Church victorious
> Shall be the Church at rest.
> —*Samuel J. Stone*

Friends
John 15:12-17

Jesus referred to those who followed him as *"friends."* The friendship to which Jesus referred is based upon the intimacy of shared knowledge. As he said, a master does not share his plans with his slaves, but he might share them with trusted friends. Shared knowledge based upon intimacy is the basis for a meaningful relationship with Sacred Presence.

Knowledge to which Jesus refers is dissimilar to knowledge that Adam and Eve sought when they disobeyed God and ate fruit from the Tree of Knowledge that the Tester said would make them like God; knowing good and evil. There is knowledge for the purpose of controlling others, and there is knowledge for the benefit of friends. Both provide personal gratification even though they serve different purposes.

The benefit of knowledge that controls is limited to the physical world where things can be measured, defined, arranged, and recycled. Jesus, on the other hand, shares intimate knowledge of God with his friends for their benefit. There no longer is need for them to climb a mountain, penetrate a cloud, or go behind a curtain to be intimate with Sacred Presence. Jesus said, *"All that I have heard from my Father I have made known to you."* Results are lasting when they evolve from an intimate relationship with God.

Have we trials and temptations?
Is there trouble anywhere?
We should never be discouraged;
Take it to the Lord in prayer.
Can we find a friend so faithful
Who will all our sorrows share?
Jesus knows our every weakness;
Take it to the Lord in Prayer.
—*Joseph M. Scriven*

BEHAVIOR IS THE LANGUAGE OF FAITH!

186

Covenant Of Blessing
Ezekiel 34:25-31

E zekiel was a religious leader with a message of hope for an enslaved nation living in a foreign land. He pictured people's daily existence as living *"with a bar and a yolk."* He vowed that freedom was in their future. Deliverance would be an act of God for the purpose of placing them under a covenant that would make them a blessing to all people and provide safety and security in their new life. The living conditions of this new covenant community would be freedom from slavery, freedom from hunger, elimination of national insults by others, and knowledge that *"God is with them."*

Evidence of the new covenant of blessing is very materialistic, and it is anchored firmly in a meaningful relationship with God. The prophetic message is clear that when God delivers the oppressed, he places them under responsibility to respond to the oppression and needs of others in a similar manner. Every generation has people who *"live with a bar and a yolk."* Blessings from God come with the promise that *"I am with you..."* The expectation is that those who have been blessed with relief will become a blessing to those in bondage, to those who are unsafe and insecure, to those who are hungry, and to those subjected to daily insults.

The task Thy wisdom hath assigned,
O let me cheerfully fulfill;
In all my works Thy presence find,
And prove thy good and perfect will.
—*Charles Wesley*

BEHAVIOR IS THE LANGUAGE OF FAITH!

Called And Predestined
Romans 8

No one is an expert on God. All that is known concerning God results from what He makes known in a manner that suits His purpose. Augustine: "By God alone may God be known." Yet, there are those who read Romans 8 and base their faith upon the notion that the foreknowledge of God predetermines who answers Jesus' call to repentance and reconciliation. Who is so presumptuous to claim to know the mind of God by reasoned analysis? This is a very individualistic perception of God's relationship with those whom He created in His image.

The Bible teaches that God does not want one of His children to be without Him. Therefore, he does not drift idly by while His creation moves away from His guiding presence. God makes His presence known and allows people to draw near or draw away. The only aspects of God's plan for humanity that appear predestined are His longing for humanity to desire his influence and the resulting consequences. There is no substantial evidence that Sacred Presence predetermines who will respond and how.

We read in the Genesis creation story that Adam and Eve chose to disobey God and suffered the predetermined consequences of alienation. Their fear and guilt made them hide from God, Who promptly called them out of hiding and addressed their need. They responded appropriately. As a result, God enabled them to manage their new life outside the idyllic garden of plenty. There are two facets of human and divine relations that are predetermined. One is God's initiative in having a creative relationship; the other consequences of humanity's response.

Lord, I would clasp Thy hand in mine,
Nor ever murmur or repine;
Content, whatever lot I see,
Since it is Thou that leadeth me.

188

He leadeth me! He leadeth me!
By His own hand He leadeth me:
His faithful follower I would be,
For by His hand He leadeth me.
—*Joseph H. Gilmore*

Tasted Good
I Peter 2:1-10

Peter reminds *"exiles of the Dispersion"* that proclamation of the Christian message requires development of a new taste that is good. Destructive thought and behavior should be replaced because *"you have received mercy."* The mercy of God revealed in Jesus becomes the *"cornerstone chosen and precious"* upon which believers build a new life *"out of the darkness ('of all malice, all guile, insincerity, envy, and all slander') into His marvelous light."* Followers of Jesus are called upon to acquire a new taste that reflects God's kindness.

Peter's analogy relates a changed life to a change in one's taste preferences. This is his way of letting people know that change from *"no people"* to *"God's people"* requires considerable effort. Our taste buds over time develop a conditioned set of preferences that take us directly to food we most enjoy. Paul in II Corinthians 2:12-14 writes that Christ *"through us spreads in every place the fragrance that comes from knowing him. For we are the aroma of Christ to God among those who are being saved and among those who are perishing."* *"Taste"*, referenced by Peter, and *"fragrance"*, referenced by Paul, combine to identify what we want.

"If indeed you have tasted that the Lord is good," then, it is natural to share with others what you enjoy. There is no requirement that Christians attempt to force-feed others with

food they might not like or want. However, it is kind to offer. The presentation is similar to the way food is introduced to infants. First we taste and then we offer.

> "Remember thee, and all thy pains
> And all thy love to me;
> Yea, while a breath, a pulse remains,
> I will remember thee."
> —*James Montgomery*

Hope In The Lord
Psalm 46

The Psalmist packed a lot into a few words. He reminds us that the creation provides two options: **"trust in the Lord"** or follow **"the way of the wicked."** Those who trust in the Lord serve the common good. In contrast are those who **"put their trust in Princes."** Although there are only two ways, there are multiple choices. Each choice is important because it contributes to a better way that is grounded upon hope in God's plan, or, it's a choice that **"when breath parts ...that very day plans perish."**

What does the Psalmist identify as attitudes and deeds that serve the common good? There are quite a few:

- justice for the oppressed;
- necessities for the dispossessed;
- freedom for those in bondage;
- enlightenment, encouragement, and opportunity for the downhearted;
- love for those aligned with God's purpose;
- care for the lonely and vulnerable;
- and resistance to forces of ruin and destruction.

The Psalmist Praises the Lord *"who made heaven and earth"* and *"who keeps the faith forever"* by addressing legitimate need through the devoted efforts of those who honor him.

> Thou grantest pardon through thy love;
> Thy grace alone availeth.
> Our works could ne'er our guilt remove;
> Yea, e'en the best life faileth.
> For none may boast himself of aught,
> But must confess thy grace hath wrought
> Whate'er in him is worthy.
> —*Martin Luther*

BEHAVIOR IS THE LANGUAGE OF FAITH!

Darkness And Light
Isaiah 60:1-6

The creation story in Genesis says that God created light before He created the sun. This isn't sloppy reasoning or sloppy composition. Rather, the account presents at the outset that the light which enlightens the universe emanates from the presence of the Creator—not from anything created. Isaiah appeared to have this in mind when he wrote to those who humbly acknowledge God's presence:

"Arise and shine; for your light has come, and the glory of the Lord has risen upon you."

The Bible frequently contrasts the light associated with Sacred Presence with the darkness of chaos. People are categorized as children of light or children of darkness. Children of light struggle to exhibit behavior that honor the Creator's presence in their lives. In contrast, children of darkness are famous for promoting their personal values. The Gospel of John refers to Jesus as the **"light of the world"** because he embodied the enlightenment that was in the beginning. Jesus prayed that the light that was in him would also be in those who followed him. Options are better understood when they are reduced to two: We can progress in light (creative living) or digress in darkness (return to chaos).

Light of the world, Thy beauty steals into every heart,
And glorifies with duty life's humblest, part;
Thou robest in Thy splendor the simplest ways of men,
And helpest them to render light back to Thee again.
—*John S.B. Monsell*

Disciples
John 1:35-51

Spiritual development does not start from scratch. It begins with awareness of Sacred Presence. Modern and primitive civilizations express evidence of spiritual awareness. Jesus did not begin making his pitch to a pool of godless people. The Gospel of John begins with Jesus' asking people who were already religious to become followers.

His audience was familiar with the language and concepts of the Jewish religion as evidenced by their attendance during the proclamation and baptismal events held by John the Baptizer. However, the writer makes it clear that they were not religious professionals. These first responders were respectful of each other's beliefs as evidenced by their willingness to share their perceptions and speculations concerning **"signs from God"** that verify His presence and guidance.

Jesus developed followers from among people who were predisposed to acknowledge God's involvement in human affairs. They were raw material with which God could work to implement His redemptive and transforming power. Being sensitive to Sacred Presence does not mean that one easily conforms to God's purpose for humanity. Jesus often referred to his followers as children because they never fully matured. They became more mature in faith and practice only after his death and resurrection that empowered them to grow in response to Sacred Presence.

> Lead, kindly Light, amid th' encircling gloom,
> Lead thou me on!
> The night is dark and I am far from home;
> Lead thou me on!
> Keep thou my feet; I do not ask to see
> The distant scene; one step enough for me.
> —*John Henry Newman*

A Point In Time
Matthew 4:17-22

Jesus fostered his intent to glorify God by choosing his original followers from among those who made no pretense of power through knowledge, wealth, religious piety, or government. Human weakness for gratifying destructive self-centered desires is a chronic condition. In contrast, the humanity of Jesus deferred to Sacred Presence as the power that enabled him **"to do justice, to love kindness, and to walk humbly before...God."** Jesus was baptized by John The Baptizer in response to his message of repentance. In this way Jesus

193

publicly identified with human weakness. He attributed all redemptive power to God and received the baptism of repentant sinners to make the point that *"Only God is good."* Paul later wrote that he personally *"would boast only in his weaknesses"* because God uses weakness to demonstrate how destructive desires can be redirected and managed for creative good. This does not imply that human weakness is a virtue that provides God an opportunity to show off.

All creative and restorative power is derivative. It originates with God who implements it to serve His purpose. Human power seeks personal gratification. Religion is an exceptionally fertile environment for the propagation of evil. Jesus identified priorities that reflect the Kingdom of God on earth: *"Now is the Son of Man glorified and God is glorified in him. If God is glorified in him, God will glorify the Son in himself, and will glorify him at once."*

All our lives belong to thee,
Thou our final loyalty;
Slaves are we whene'er we share
That devotion anywhere.
God of love and God of power,
Thou hast called us for this hour.
—*Gerald Kennedy*

Self-Denial
Luke 9:23-27; 57-62

The Kingdom of God on earth was embodied in Jesus' life of self-denial and humility in the presence of his Heavenly Father. Christian self-denial is a consequence of commitment and resource allocation toward cultivating thoughts and deeds that reflect favorably upon sacred influence. Self-denial glorifies God when it subordinates natural desire for personal gratification to activity that labors for the well-being of others.

Jesus taught, **"If you love those who love you, what credit is that to you? For even sinners love those who love them. If you do good to those who do good to you, what credit is that to you? For even sinners do the same. If you lend to those from whom you expect to receive, what credit is that to you? Even sinners lend to sinners, in order to receive back the same amount. But love your enemies, and do good and lend, expecting nothing in return; and your reward will be great, and you will be children of the Most High; for He Himself is kind to the ungrateful and the wicked. Be merciful, just as your Father is merciful."**

Indecisiveness is diminished by self-denial that represents a bond between God and humanity. Anyone who has ever plowed a field, or watched someone else do it, knows that a straight row results only when the one plowing never takes his eye away from the fixed point toward which he is going. A crook is made in the plowed row at every point when one looks back to see what is left behind. Jesus taught, ***"No one who puts his hand to the plow and looks back is fit for the kingdom of God."***

"Give Me thy heart," says the Father above—
No gift so precious to Him as our love;
Softly He whispers wherever thou art,
"Gratefully trust Me and give Me thy heart."
—*Eliza E. Hewett*

Chain Of Command
Matthew 10:34-43

Jesus described the perpetual conflict between good and evil as a state of war that precludes compromise. Good is creative and evil is destructive. Neither can tolerate the other. Defining good and evil can create hostility among family members where love, peace, and security are intended to provide a pleasant environment.

Jesus said that loyalty to his revelation of God's will and purpose on earth is important enough to risk family disruption and alienation between neighbors. When human will is in bondage to Sacred Presence, there are two inevitable consequences. First is genuine concern for the legitimate needs of others, and second is humility in one's relationship with God.

Behavioral motivations that gratify personal desires are difficult to override because they are natural and well-developed. This makes "Thy will or my will" a continuously discordant environment to manage. Paul wrote in Romans 7:15, *"I do not understand my own actions. For I do not do what I want, but I do the very thing I hate."* Sacred Presence persists in encouraging conformity to divine influence and empowers participation in the new creation with Jesus as the second Adam.

Lo! the hosts of evil 'round us,
Scorn thy Christ, assail his ways!
From the fears that long have bound us,
Free our hearts to faith and praise.
Grant us wisdom, grant us courage,
For the living of these days,
For the living of these days.
—*Harry Emerson Fosdick*

BEHAVIOR IS THE LANGUAGE OF FAITH!

Restoration
Psalm 128

The Psalmist speaks from a deep conviction that *"the fear of God is the beginning of wisdom..."* The Power that created the universe is entitled to be feared. Whatever Power might be, it is first and foremost the force that is in control. It is reasonable that nothing in the universe has any basis for claiming comparable status.

Adam and Eve challenged the Creator. According to the creation account with which the Psalmist was familiar, this arrogant challenge generated consequences. Barred from the comfort and tranquility of an idyllic garden, Adam had to work and sweat for a living, Eve was given pain in childbirth, and their children—Cain and Abel—were plagued with jealousy that resulted in Abel's death.

The Psalmist announced that the only effective corrective measure to overcome this dysfunctional human condition is a return to basic belief in the awesome power and influence of the Creator. Only then will His Sacred Presence be given proper attention. The Poet anticipated happy and productive work, a pleasurable and fruitful family life, and a joyous communal religious experience. Regardless of how specific situations play out, attention is directed to the influential power of God as the solid foundation upon which to construct one's life.

For why? The Lord our God is good,
His mercy is forever sure;
His truth at all times firmly stood,
And shall from age to age endure.
—*William Kethe*

BEHAVIOR IS THE LANGUAGE OF FAITH!

The Source
Matthew 19:16-30

Wealth and legalistic religion have always been joined at the hip. Excellence in both aspects of life is personally challenging and requires ability and discipline. The Gospel of Matthew puts wealth and legalistic religion in proper perspective by reporting an exchange between Jesus and a wealthy religious young man. The young man approached Jesus, whom he recognized as a man of God, asking, *"Teacher what good deed must I do to have eternal life?"* The question implies a prerequisite ability that empowers one to perfect goodness by acquisition of knowledge of what is good. This is a common misperception that Jesus corrected by saying, *"There is only one who is good."* Therefore, "good" is not a condition that is applied to humans. From beginning to end, life is a tutorial by which humanity is made aware of goodness that eludes full actualization.

The young man's management of wealth and religious laws created an illusion of power that generated enthusiasm to know and master anything that might be missing. He made it plain to Jesus, *"All these I have kept. What do I still lack?"* Jesus challenged his pride of possession and religious accomplishment by telling him to put both aside and follow him in a life controlled and managed by the Sacred Presence of one who alone is good. He sorrowfully refused. Jesus wanted him to be rid of those things that prevented him from recognizing his weakness because God is honored when his Sacred Presence transforms life *"to do justice, and to love kindness, and to walk humbly with your God."* Jesus was blunt and to the point. The narrative implies that the young man intended this to be a single information-seeking encounter without any suggestion of intimate long-term involvement. The familiar combination of wealth and legalistic religion is a savage addiction that propagates toxic arrogance. For this reason Jesus warns us, *"It is easier for a camel to go through the eye of a needle than for someone who is rich (in wealth and self-*

righteousness) to enter the kingdom of God." The Kingdom of Heaven is modeled. The Laws of Moses are taught.

Who can become part of *"Thy kingdom come, thy will be done on earth as it is in heaven?"* Human arrogance and pride must realize it is impossible. However, *"with God all things are possible"* for those who place human weakness on the altar in submission to His transforming sacred presence. Paul in II Corinthians 12:9 wrote that the Lord's message to him was, *"My grace is sufficient for you, for my power is made perfect in weakness."* God is honored and glorified by the Kingdom of Heaven He builds on earth utilizing bent nails and crooked boards.

> O Father, deign these walls to bless;
> Fill with thy love their emptiness,
> And let their door a gateway be
> To lead us from ourselves to thee.
> —*John Greenleaf Whittier*

BEHAVIOR IS THE LANGUAGE OF FAITH!

Encounter
Isaiah 6:1-8

Every genuine religious experience acknowledges the holiness of God to whom we draw near or from whom we drift away. Isaiah described his spiritual experience using the most beautiful imagery. He was overwhelmed with a sense of God's holiness which made him aware of his own profane nature. God responded, burned away his infection, and blotted out his imperfections. In gratitude, Isaiah volunteered to tell others of God's kindness and redeeming power.

The existence of a burden is obviously prerequisite to life-changing relief when the burden is lifted. A journey through the dreaded *"valley of the shadow of death"* causes the traveler to cry out for relief. The combination of guilt, regret, and reprieve results in gratitude.

In 1958, I was minister to four rural churches in southeastern North Carolina. One of my early challenges was to encourage local preachers of numerous denominations to join in a ministerial association. While making my rounds, I located Pastor Raymond putting out fertilizer in a plowed field where he planned to set out tobacco. He stopped his tractor at the end of the row where I was waiting. We engaged in idle chatter before I stated my business. He agreed to listen. Before I left, he gave testimony to his Christian faith. He said that he never learned to read and write. His wife read the Bible to him every night, after which he formulated in his mind the sermon for the coming Sunday. He would recite his Scripture lesson from memory before he preached.

After that brief personal history, he said, "Brother Ed, if you were flat on the ground between these tobacco rows with four bags of fertilizer on top of you, could you get up?" I said, "No." He continued; "If I reached down and rolled each bag off of you would you feel the burden lifted?" I said, "Yes" His voice softened when he said, "That's the way it was with me when God forgave my sins and lifted the burden of guilt from my life. I rejoice to tell others who are burdened that Jesus brings the message of relief."

The relief message of Isaiah, Pastor Raymond, and others is meaningless to those who are not similarly burdened and debilitated. To all who are weighted down, there is good news that the Creator of the universe built in a means for relief. He sears the wound, kills the infection, overlooks the scar, and receives us as unblemished. That's something worth sharing.

His yoke is easy;
His burden is light.
I've found it so.
He leadeth me by day and by night
Where living waters flow.
—R.E. Hudson

BEHAVIOR IS THE LANGUAGE OF FAITH!

Complete The Task
Colossians 4:2-18

What would you expect to read in a letter from a friend in prison? Would the content be anything like what the Christian community received from Paul who was imprisoned in Rome? He expressed concern that they thank God for the changes in their lives and for their opportunities to share effectively the mysteries of Christ with others.

People of faith are challenged continuously to present **"the mystery of Christ"** in a sensible and meaningful way to outsiders. There is strong inclination to package faith to conform to the tastes and fashions of insiders who are comforted by revisiting heartwarming impressions presented in familiar language.

Paul writes that some important characteristics of Christian witness that might be meaningful to outsiders are *"wise conduct," "making the most of time,"* and *"gracious speech,"* all of which, he said, are as permanent as salt. Paul's Christian jail-mates added their prayer that the Colossian community of faith be *"mature"* and *"assured"* in their testimony. Christians witness to faith. We do not argue fact. Can it be too often repeated that "we never get a second opportunity to make a first impression?"

> O'er all the world thy spirit send,
> And make thy goodness known,
> Till earth and heaven together blend
> Their praises at thy throne.
> —*Ray Palmer*

BEHAVIOR IS THE LANGUAGE OF FAITH!

Cast In Deep Water
Luke 5:1-11

Jesus used what was understood and did something with it that was not understood. He invited those present to participate in changing their view of the meaning and purpose of life that was authenticated by what they saw him do. After he got their attention, he offered a new mold for revising behavior. Luke gives us a simple visual tutorial in which the presence of Jesus made something productive that was unproductive without him.

The process of change cannot be defined adequately or measured according to natural law. Clearly, Jesus was not caught up in an ongoing commercial fishing enterprise, nor did the fishermen see it as such. They did not pool their resources and buy additional fishing equipment in anticipation of repeat performances. Instead, they followed him, even though their understanding was limited and their performance was grossly inadequate. Sacred Presence confronts human limitations with the suggestion that we *"cast our nets in deeper water"* as a new arrangement that encourages humility and reliance upon sacred influence to serve the *"common good."*

> I need thy presence every passing hour.
> What but thy grace can foil the tempter's power?
> Who, like thyself, my guide and stay can be?
> Through cloud and sunshine,
> Lord, abide with me.
> —Henry F. Lyte

BEHAVIOR IS THE LANGUAGE OF FAITH!

Adversity Before Deliverance
Acts 27:21-26

Paul was on a missionary journey to Rome to deliver the good news of God's reconciling forgiveness when a storm threatened to sink the ship at sea. At Paul's insistence, the captain scuttled the boat and saved the occupants. The apparent reason this account was recorded in Acts was to stress that adversity and delay are not reasons to forsake commitment to purpose. Paul did not expect God to exempt him from adversity. He accepted whatever occurred and adjusted his itinerary. In his letter to the church in Phillip, Paul wrote, *"I can do all things through him who strengthens me."*

It is commonplace for the Bible to report on circumstances where adversity precedes deliverance. Life begins with countless sperm struggling in the womb to become first to fertilize an egg and create life. Unsuccessful sperm are eliminated from the creative process. Overcoming adversity, in a variety of forms, naturally and predictably precedes fulfillment. It is important to understand the creative process presented in the Bible wherein testing is built into the system. One could make the case that God's creative power is tested continually by the resistant forces of chaos and darkness. In his image, we are presented an identical challenge. His Sacred Presence gives us a powerful support system that influences our responses, forgives our weaknesses, and inspires our continued effort.

When through fiery trials thy pathways lie,
My grace, all sufficient, shall be thy supply;
The flame shall not hurt thee; I only design
Thy dross to consume, and thy gold to refine.
—*Early American Hymn*

203

Lonely And Afflicted
Psalm 25

The path of loneliness and affliction is congested and well-worn. The Psalmist presents God as the best option for those who feel pain and despair too great for them to endure. His appeal is void of pride and pretense and is based upon anticipation of God's kindness and love toward those who come to Him as a humble child. Being teachable is an enormous advantage along the pathway of a meaningful relationship with the Creator. We find it difficult to think about God's purpose when personal interests do not embrace Him.

This Psalm highlights humility that enables personal gratification to become subservient to, and compatible with, God's purpose. Spiritual awareness is an aspect of life that we need in order to give enduring meaning and purpose to all that surrounds us. We properly respond to God's resourcefulness by learning and applying; God is glorified.

And so the yearning strong,
With which the soul will long,
Shall far outpass the power of human telling;
For none can guess its grace,
Till he become the place
Wherein the Holy Spirit makes His dwelling
—*Bianco Da Siena*

BEHAVIOR IS THE LANGUAGE OF FAITH!

In My Body
Philippians 1:19-30

Jesus said, *"The Father and I are one...I seek to do not my own will but the will of Him who sent me...Only God is good...He who has seen me has seen the Father."* These would be words of arrogance except, **"He did not count equality with God a thing to be grasped, but emptied himself and became an obedient servant..."** Faith in Jesus as the Son of God includes acceptance of his physical presentation of the Creator of the universe. God's sacred presence triumphs over chaotic evil by granting to all who receive Him the privilege of doing good **"on earth as it is done in heaven."**

God imposes Himself upon humanity which is forced to process the experience. Nothing happens unless perception and thought find emotional support **("Out of the believer's heart shall flow rivers of living *water."*)** Perception, thought, and emotion activate the body, and in the words of the Gospel of John, *"The Word became flesh and lived among us, and we have seen His glory, the glory as of a Father's only son, full of grace and truth."* The alternative path is unambiguously described by the writer of Ecclesiastes, *"So, I hated life, because of what was done under the sun was grievous to me; for all is vanity and chasing after the wind."*

The summary prayer of Jesus is recorded in John 17:21, **"...that they may all be one. As you, Father, are in me and I am in you, may they also be in us, so that the world may believe that you have sent me."** These words follow the natural pathway through perception, thought, and emotion, culminating in **"fruits of the Spirit." (Galatians 5:22-23)**

> I would be true, for there are those who trust me;
> I would be pure, for there are those who care;
> I would be strong, for there is much to suffer;
> I would be brave, for there is much to dare,
> I would be brave for there is much to dare.
> —*Howard A. Walter*

205

As I Do
John 13:1-20

In the upper room with his disciples, Jesus wordlessly taught that behavior is the language of faith. Peter objected to the lesson when his teacher performed as a servant. After a brief exchange, Jesus continued; it was necessary for all of the disciples to understand personally the body language of faith.

Jesus asked his disciples, **"Do you know what I have done?"** The question customarily asked by a teacher is, "Do you understand what I said?" In the language of faith, what is done takes precedence over what is said. Jesus defined the pathway of discipleship—*"If you know these things, you are blessed if you do them."*

Words are the currency of civilization that enables people to share knowledge and understanding. The body language of faith makes a statement concerning one's relationship with Sacred Presence. When Jesus washed and dried the feet of his disciples, he conveyed to them, and to all who know of the event, a message from God. Inspired behavior of believers continues to be the preferred means for communicating God's life-changing forgiveness to those who feel the need to experience it.

Inspire the living faith which whosoe'er receive,
the witness in themselves they have and consciously believe,
the faith that conquers all, and doth the mountain move,
and saves whoe'er on Jesus call, and perfects them in love.
—*Charles Wesley*

BEHAVIOR IS THE LANGUAGE OF FAITH!

Kingdom Is Near
Mark 1:15

Jesus revealed God's sacred Kingdom in a profane environment with an elaborate system of religious codes propagated by a hierarchy of priests and rabbis who played bit parts. It was profane because it was incapable of being otherwise. Institutional religion was never intended to be center stage; however, a supporting cast is necessary to set the stage for the Central Character.

Over many generations supporting actors embellished their roles and the Central Character became primarily valued for His name on the marquee. The play became a drama of anticipation rather than fulfillment. God's Leading Man was assigned the permanent role of The One Who Is Coming. With minimum fanfare, the Director placed the Main Character (Jesus of Nazareth) on stage with a radical message that the preliminaries were over and all attention must be centered upon him. The *"good news"* unfolded as he played out his assigned role destined from the beginning, *"...Thy will be done on earth as it is in heaven."*

Jesus' opening lines mean nothing apart from what he said and did for the time he remained on stage. He subordinated to God, and served others. He performed in sharp contrast to the secondary actors who relentlessly embellished their roles. Jesus revealed the Kingdom of God through his devotion to God and his commitment to the well-being of the others.

O'er all those wide extended plains
Shines one eternal day;
There God the Son forever reigns,
And scatters night away.
No chilling winds, nor poisonous breath,
Can reach that healthful shore;
Sickness and sorrow, pain and death,
Are felt and feared no more.
—*Samuel Stennett*

If You Choose
Mark 1:40-45

Mark, Matthew, and Luke present the same details surrounding the leper's cleansing. The leper doesn't express any doubt in the ability of Jesus to make him clean. His confidence in Jesus, and his life as a shunned unclean person, contributed to his decision to let Jesus decide about his cleansing. The three Gospel writers wanted the world to know that a leprous man of faith presented himself to Jesus and his condition changed.

The leper set a procedural precedent early in Mark's account by presenting his debilitating problem to Jesus as one who exhibited the power and control of God over body and spirit. Everyone has issues that need to be addressed, some more evident and debilitating than others. Sacred Presence customizes response to human conditions and does not conform to manipulation. The leper's demeanor and words deferred to Jesus when he said, *"If you choose..."*

Jesus did not present God in a box available on demand to conform to the whims and caprices of those whom he created. Rather, he revealed the results of *"seeking first the Kingdom of God and His righteousness..."* in order for created things to be properly arranged and managed. *"Thy will be done on earth as it is in heaven..."* is a humble request by people of faith, not an empty request for a disembodied experience.

Strong Son of God, immortal love,
Whom we, that have not seen Thy face,
By faith, and faith alone, embrace,
Believing where we cannot prove.
—*Alfred Tennyson*

Show Yourself As Testimony
Mark 1:40-45

Institutional religion serves a great number of people with varying levels of interest, some of whom might otherwise not relate to an unstructured arrangement. Jesus healed, and thereby cleansed, a leper, who under Jewish law was considered unclean and was not permitted to enter the Temple. After cleansing the leper, Jesus instructed him to go to the Temple and present his cleansed body to the priest. He was then to make an offering consistent with the laws of Moses as a public witness for those who had received a blessing from God.

Jesus never abandoned institutional religion. He folds his **"good news"** of God's redemptive forgiveness into religious ritual that serves a critical universal need. This event is consistent with Jesus' insistence that he came to fulfill Law, ritual, and expectation, not destroy them. The majority of our beloved teachings of Jesus are quotes from the Law, Psalms, and Prophets of the Old Testament. However, Jesus taught that new wine should be put in new wineskins with the understanding that old wineskins and new wineskins exhibit the same process.

> Millions of souls, in glory now,
> Were fed and feasted here;
> And millions more, still on the way,
> Around the board appear.
> —*Philip Doddridge*

BEHAVIOR IS THE LANGUAGE OF FAITH!

Religion And Government
Psalms 2 and Acts 4:23-31

The connection between religion and government has been around as long as the two have existed. Reading Psalms 2, we find that David is accepted by Israel as God's anointed ruler. David's political adversaries did not accept his claim of divine endorsement, authority, and purpose. They made alliances to war against him. David's response was to guarantee that he would be victorious because he had God's designation— *"You are my son...I will make nations your heritage...and the earth your possessions...break them with iron...dash them like a vessel."*

Kings and nations are prone to arrogance when they view themselves as fulfilling God's purpose, even when consistently warned to *"serve God with fear and trembling... or ...perish."* Earthly rulers have a long tradition of skillfully equating their powerful positions with divine purpose. When their subjects buy into this idea, the result is mass loyalty willing to fight and die for their king. One need never, for one moment, forget that the ruler/religion connection is ancient.

When we shift from Psalms 2 and read Acts 4:23-31, we find that Jesus, a man of **"justice and kindness,"** is God's anointed who serves and heals rather than conquer and destroy. Political power, in the Christian tradition, can never again legitimately finesse God to re-designate them as his anointed to **"break and dash"** in his name while serving their own purpose and benefit.

Soldiers of Christ, arise,
and put your armor on,
Strong in the strength which God supplies
through His eternal Son.
Strong in the Lord of hosts,
and in His mighty power,
Who in the strength of Jesus trusts
is more than conqueror.
—*Charles Wesley*

Behave Yourself
John 3:16

Nicodemus was a prominent Pharisee who had a private night meeting with Jesus. He began by acknowledging the presence of God in Jesus' life as evidenced by exceptional things Jesus did. Pharisees did not attempt to be exceptional. They were noted for their meticulous management of religious laws that affected ordinary daily activities. Over the centuries their dedicated study and consultation resulted in multiple commandments guiding behavior.

Jesus' response to Nicodemus presented a clear picture of what is required to function in a relationship where God is king. *"No one can see the kingdom of God without being born from above."* Rebirth entails a new way of relating and a new language. The new relationship honors God's dominion and power, as in *"Thy kingdom come. Thy will be done on earth as it is in heaven."* The new medium of communication is behavior that is the language of infants, as in *"Whoever does not receive the kingdom of God as a little child will never enter it."* Because words are not available, the only way an infant expresses itself is through behavior referred to as body language. Words come later and are best used for analysis and evaluation. Maximum clarity of expression is achieved through behavior that is also the language of faith.

Jesus, thy boundless love to me
No thought can reach, no tongue declare;
Unite my thankful heart with thee,
And reign without a rival there.
To Thee above, dear Lord, I live;
Myself to Thee, dear Lord, I give.
—*Paul Gerhardt*

Three Pillars
Acts 24:24-27

P aul was accused of insurrection and was granted a hearing before Roman governor Felix. Paul's presentation was brief as he focused upon the essentials of his Christian faith. Felix was married to a Jew so he was familiar with Jewish beliefs. This enabled Paul to avoid explaining detailed Jewish theology before presenting the heart of his message that had universal application.

Justice was Paul's first foundation pillar. Everyone with political authority has some concept of justice whether they apply it or not. So Paul began his testimony before Felix with reference to the importance of treating people fairly. Justice is not conditioned by whether or not we like or are emotionally attached to another person. What is important is that others be given the same consideration as one would like to be given.

"Love your neighbor as yourself", references unconditional justice. Justice is applied to the unlovable as well as the loveable. The laws of our nation are based upon justice that stipulates innocence until proven guilty because it minimizes verdicts based upon personal bias or preconceived notions. Justice is the difference between an old-time lynching and a legal hanging. The end result might be the same, but the accused is treated fairly when a jury renders the *verdict*.

Justice is no guarantee of correct evaluations, and it is for this reason that we say God alone is one hundred percent just in His judgments. The gospel challenges believers to reflect God's justice. The Bible teaches that the more sensitive we are to God's sacred presence, the more just we are in our relations with others, and the less likely we are to make our own peculiarities the basis for evaluating others.

Self-control is the second foundation pillar upon which Paul builds. Self-control is concerned with managing ourselves. Justice is concerned with managing relationships with others. Paul wanted Felix to know that Christians receive the gift of God's sacred presence and power that enables patient consideration of words and deeds that are mutually beneficial. Christians know it is not enough to be accurate in analyzing what is right and wrong behavior. Most important is thoughtfully and patiently developing a way to relate to others so they too might be drawn into a greater awareness of God's redemptive presence. Jesus taught, **"Blessed are the merciful..."** Mercy evolves out of self-control when we manage and train our brain to reflect Sacred Presence rather than selfish preferences.

Judgment is the third foundation pillar that Paul set before Felix. The Bible teaches, **"The fear of the Lord is the beginning of wisdom."** Every living thing comes to an end, and it is unwise to live arrogantly as though we are in control. Living under the judgment of God's justice is the basis for hope unless we prefer to reach the end and go it alone. Gratitude is what Christians bring to judgment because we believe that only by faith in God's redeeming grace as revealed in Jesus will we appear before the throne of judgment and be found worthy. The three foundation pillars are: just treatment of others, management of self, and reliance upon God's sacred presence. Altering the design to accommodate personal eccentricities is counterproductive.

Think on these things...

Don was an acquaintance of mine whose hobby was building small aircraft in his workshop behind his house. His love for a challenge led him to build a "pusher" which he had never done before. It was a small two-passenger plane where the rear occupant had to slide his feet and legs under the front passenger in order to fit in place.

The plane was so sensitive that Don asked a very skilled pilot friend to test fly it for him. They followed procedures and the plane passed with flying colors. Don wanted to begin another challenge so he advertized and sold his "pusher" to a man in Texas.

A year later Don received a visit from a representative of the FAA telling him the plane crashed killing both occupants. There was no indication that he did anything wrong; however, investigation was routine. Don learned that the plane's owner had shifted the ballast, which maintained balance, in order to accommodate an overweight friend. Witnesses said the plane got about a hundred feet in the air and then crashed killing both occupants.

BEHAVIOR IS THE LANGUAGE OF FAITH!

God's Children
Mark 10:13-16

Children provided Jesus with an effective instructional aid concerning the kingdom of heaven because they communicate their desires primarily through behavior rather than words. Also, children haven't developed **"hardness of heart"** to a level that is difficult to overcome. Jesus taught that evidence of the kingdom of heaven on earth is behavioral rather than verbal. The kingdom of heaven was revealed effectively in the life of Jesus because his behavior was consistent with his words.

John Wesley was fond of the phrase "growing in grace" to describe the presence and power of God that progressively enables words of faith to be implemented by the community of faith. A poem that begins with the words "I'd rather see a sermon than hear one any day. I'd rather one would walk with me than merely show the way." is illustrative of the fact that verbal skills never catch up with behavior as primary means of communicating the Christian good news of God's transforming forgiveness. Jesus explained nothing to the children. *"He put his hands on them and blessed them."*

'Tis mystery all: th' Immortal dies:
Who can explore His strange design?
In vain the firstborn seraph tries
To sound the depths of love divine.
'Tis mercy all! Let earth adore;
Let angel minds inquire no more.
—*Charles Wesley*

BEHAVIOR IS THE LANGUAGE OF FAITH!

Impossible Possibility
Mark 10:17-31

Jesus admired the dedication and discipline of a prosperous man who kept the commandments from his youth. His religious awareness enabled him to recognize Jesus as "good teacher." Yet, there was something lacking in his spiritual development that prompted him to ask **"What must I do to inherit eternal life?"** Use of the word "inherit" suggests a level of spiritual maturity which recognized that eternal life is a gift. Even so, he remained anxious that something remained for him to do to be worthy of the inheritance.

Jesus touched upon the man's wealth as a possible hindrance to the assurance he was seeking. This suggestion was inconsistent with the commonly-held belief in that culture that wealth and good health were signs of God's approval. We recall that when a man blind from birth was brought to Jesus for healing, the question was asked as to whose sin caused the blindness. Jesus' answered that sin did not cause the condition. This ran contrary to prevailing religious teaching. It is not surprising that the prosperous man sadly turned and walked away because he hoped Jesus would respond in a manner consistent with tradition.

Jesus made the point that God alone is good. Achieving the kingdom of heaven by being good is not an option. The arrogance of such a way of thinking is an impediment to an attitude of humility that enables one to receive the kingdom as a gift of God who shares His goodness with all who recognize and desire it.

The commandments are a gift of God's grace that teaches the limitations of human will. The kingdom of heaven is God's gift of grace that does not judge according to human limitations. **"Blessed are the poor in spirit for theirs is the Kingdom of Heaven."**

"Thou grantest pardon through thy love;
Thy grace alone availeth.
Our works could ne'er our guilt remove;
Yea, e'en the best of life faileth.
For none may boast himself of aught,
But must confess thy grace hath wrought
Whate'er in him is worthy."
—*Martin Luther*

Rule Or Serve
Mark 10:35-45

The Bible presents a contrast between earthly and heavenly values that is difficult to take in. Power and control dominate the earthly scene. Their avenues of expression are many and complex. Surprisingly, Jesus clarifies and simplifies the preferred path with a single word—**"servant."** God controlled and Jesus served. Those who follow Jesus should do the same. Jesus did not display a desire for special

216

consideration, as expressed by James and John, because it was an inappropriate demonstration of arrogance. Instead, he redirected them toward the one thing he had to offer— "servitude."

Jesus placed himself at odds with self-seeking desire to control. Instead he worked for the *"common good"* done in God's name. Jesus did not die in a quest for secular conquest. He glorified his Heavenly Father and endured the consequences.

> One Lord, in one great name
> Unite us all who own thee;
> Cast out our pride and shame
> That hinder to enthrone thee;
> The world has waited long,
> Has travailed long in pain;
> To heal its ancient wrong,
> Come, Prince of Peace and reign.
> —George W. Briggs

BEHAVIOR IS THE LANGUAGE OF FAITH!

Another King
Acts 17:1-9

Paul argued in the Thessalonian Synagogue that the resurrection of Jesus from the dead was God's validation of his messianic role. The general public and government authorities were disinterested as long as the argument was a religious matter presented in the synagogue. However, Paul expanded his audience to those Gentiles who had an interest. Devout Greeks and several leading women became converts. Social unrest followed and Christian converts became known as *"people who turned the world upside down."* Government authorities considered this a direct challenge to the emperor.

Secular authorities are well acquainted with the practical application of Jesus' observation that **"no man serves two masters."** Eventually, serious religious conviction conflicts with secular values, customs, and established authority. When this happens, power acts to suppress. Christ in conflict with culture is normal. Take care!

Rise up O men of God!
Have done with lesser things.
Give heart and mind and soul and strength
To serve the King of kings.
—*William P. Merrill*

Donkey Ride
Mark 11:1-11

Jesus consolidates his message and his life into one dramatic event. The scene began when he rode into Jerusalem on an unbroken donkey. This was interpreted by the crowd, which shouted *"Hosanna"* (save now), as initiating the return of the Kingdom of David as prophesied in Zechariah 9:9. The life and teachings of Jesus did not coincide with the crowd's response. They wanted a powerful leader to free them from Rome. The power revealed in Jesus overcomes estrangement between Creator and created. His unadorned purpose is fulfilled as a humble obedient servant of his heavenly Father.

The need for us to follow Jesus is understood better when we acknowledge his humanity. We gaze at him from a distance when we reverence him as an icon elevated to an unnatural category. Jesus, as icon, places less immediate practical demands upon his followers than when he is a fellow traveler along difficult roads with multiple options for good or evil. Our

218

"Deliverer" rode on a donkey, was crowned with thorns, and died on a cross. *"Therefore God has highly exalted him and bestowed on him the name that is above every name..."* *(Philippians 2:9)*

Must Jesus bear the cross alone,
And all the world go free?
No, there's a cross for everyone,
And there's a cross for me.
—*Thomas Shepherd*

BEHAVIOR IS THE LANGUAGE OF FAITH!

Tenants
Mark 12:1-12

Some view life as a gift, some as an entitlement, and others as an unpleasant experience from birth. The Parable of the Vineyard and Tenants is about the first two, wherein an opportunity was treated as an entitlement that escalated into an attempt to establish control. People who adopt a false sense of identity are destined to engage in activities for which they are incapable. The results are unrewarding. Poor choices result in accountability for undesirable consequences.

The parable described contemporary religious leaders who had all of the institutional tools available to serve the common good. Yet, they lost sight of God's purpose and arranged for their own positions of prominence and power. They lost sight of creation as a gift. The appropriate response should have been gratitude that desires a relationship with the giver which reflects his will and purpose. Augustine reminds us, "Thou hast made

219

us for thyself, O Lord, and our hearts are restless until they find their rest in thee"

Open my eyes, that I may see
Glimpses of truth Thou hast for me;
Place in my hands the wonderful key
That shall unclasp and set me free.
Silently now I wait for Thee,
Ready my God, Thy will to see.
Open my eyes, illumine me,
Spirit divine!
—*Clara H. Scott*

BEHAVIOR IS THE LANGUAGE OF FAITH!

God Provides Structure
Mark 12:12-17

When God created structure, He included religion and government, both of which He made accountable within their assigned boundaries. Jesus was appreciative and supportive of religious and political institutions for the service they provide for the common good. He participated in Temple worship and recommended it to others. He recognized the benefit of government that provided safety and stability, and He strongly suggested that people pay their taxes. Institutional imperfection is not a sound basis for avoiding taxes.

Organized religion provides structure that enables participants to relate and communicate with one another about spiritual experiences. Religious institutional imperfection is not a sound basis for avoiding voluntary participation and contribution. Jesus worked within the prevailing structures to

220

elevate them to their highest and best purpose by seeking the common good. The Bible teaches that every person is tested continually for godliness in accordance with the variety of gifts, abilities, and beliefs that are inspired by the same Spirit. Religious authorities were attempting to make Jesus appear as a political insurrectionist who opposed the Roman Emperor. Jesus finessed the situation by prioritizing a relationship with God while acknowledging the limited function of government to maintain order. Paul echoed this understanding when he wrote to the Corinthian church, *"we live as human beings, but we do not wage war according to human standards."*

O Lord and Master of us all,
Whate'er our name or sign,
We own Thy sway, We hear Thy call,
We test our lives by Thine.
—*John G. Whittier*

BEHAVIOR IS THE LANGUAGE OF FAITH!

Resurrection
Mark 12:18-27

Jesus addressed the dispute concerning resurrection of the dead by referencing the scriptures and the power of God. These are the only common-sense references available for the community of faith when it comes to life after death.

The scriptures provide accounts of how quality people think and act. The idea is that people who creatively influence society to do good are forever preserved as important components of the universal creative process. People usually have sense enough to preserve thoughts and deeds that are recognized as beneficial.

The basis for resurrection is the Creator who preserves what He values. He puts eternity in the minds of humans without full disclosure. It is not important that we know the details. It is important that the Creator knows the details. On earth, we have more than enough to occupy our time and talents without attempting to manage eternity.

> Abide with me from morn till eve,
> For without Thee I cannot live;
> Abide with me when night is nigh,
> For without Thee I dare not die.
> —*John Keble*

BEHAVIOR IS THE LANGUAGE OF FAITH!

Two Commandments
Mark 12:28-34

How often do we seek answers only to learn they are in plain view? This is the situation in our scripture lesson where a religious leader asked Jesus to specify the greatest commandment. It is worth noting that there are Ten Commandments from Moses and hundreds of derivatives that developed over time. To ask Jesus' opinion about the greatest was a test because the Pharisees taught that no one commandment was greater than another. Jesus' response combined Deuteronomy 6:4 and Leviticus 19:18 into a two-fold summary which surpassed the detailed itemization of laws that attempted to cover every aspect of daily life.

The Bible contains many variations of the basic question, **"What must I do?"** The emphasis is consistently upon the personal pronoun "I." Jesus presented a combination that emphasized devotion to God, who gives life, and concern for one's neighbor, with whom life is shared. These prioritized foci can be learned from childhood. The "I" distorts understanding.

> Follow with reverent steps the great example of him
> whose holy work was doing good;
> so shall the wide earth seem our Father's temple,
> each loving life a psalm of gratitude.
> —*John Greenleaf Whittier*

BEHAVIOR IS THE LANGUAGE OF FAITH!

Reliable Witness
Acts 1:12-26 (Psalm 109:8)

Judas died following his betrayal of Jesus. The disciples believed that Psalm 109:8 was a mandate for them to name a replacement who was with Jesus from the beginning of his ministry through the resurrection. The purpose of such a credentialed replacement was to provide an authentic witness to all that had occurred. There was no apparent attempt to initiate an institutional power structure; they just simply caste lots between two qualified candidates as their method of relying upon divine influence.

The process and the replacement was intended to provide the most reliable eye witness to the signs Jesus did that authenticated, according to Jewish religious tradition, the power of God at work in word and deed. The process from destructive to creative living for the common good continues to provide the most reliable witness to Sacred Presence.

There was a seafood vender in the nineteen eighties that had a sign on the shoulder of highway 17 in North Carolina that read, "Louisiana Oysters fifteen dollars a bushel." The evening news reported a Health Department warning about contaminated Louisiana Oysters. Over-night the sign was replaced with one that read, "Texas Oysters fifteen dollars a bushel." Changing labels without changing content is not reliable testimony for edible oysters or Christian behavior.

> "The seas shall waste, the skies in smoke decay,
> Rocks fall to dust, and mountains waste away;
> But fixed His word, His saving power remains;
> Thy realm shall last, thy own Messiah reigns!"
> —*Alexander Pope*

BEHAVIOR IS THE LANGUAGE OF FAITH!

Lying To God
Acts 5:1-11

Appearing to be something we are not is a common flaw that is destructive because of the way it affects others. When the deception involves religion, the harm is magnified because God's influence is misrepresented. People naturally attempt to shield themselves from people who misrepresent themselves for personal gain. However, the misrepresentation of God's influential presence is more than an indiscretion. It is a sin against the Holy Spirit because good and evil are mislabeled and people are harmed. It is destructive to imply or claim to reflect a creative relationship with Sacred Presence when none exists.

God does not force himself upon his children. He has made himself known, and we can choose to live with him or without him. People of faith must behave in a manner that favorably reflects Sacred Influence, and rely upon God's grace to overpower the flaws. Jesus taught that no one serves two masters. Behavior is expected to identify who is serving whom.

> "Christ leads me through no darker rooms
> Than he went through before;
> He that into God's kingdom comes
> Must enter by this door."
> —*Richard Baxter*

BEHAVIOR IS THE LANGUAGE OF FAITH!

Two Of Us
Matthew 6:1-24

Jesus teaches that relationships with God are private and become public through behavior. Theists, too frequently, equate evidence of their convictions with public display of tutorial institutional tools and codified performance evaluation criteria. Jesus acknowledges that there is a pay-off in public religious display. He also points out that the ego gratification derived from the display of cultured religious activity routinely results from accommodation with the values of **"the kingdom of this world."** Personal public piety is its own reward. Payment is not received twice for the same investment.

The reward system administered by God is understood as private, and is based upon service that God motivates and empowers. Personal piety is derivative because prayer, sacrifice, and charity are fruit-bearing results of God's involvement, including his discrete reward system. The design of creation appears to function at the highest level when effort is directed toward God's glory exemplified by the life and teachings of Jesus who reminded us that **"no one serves two masters."**

"Still to the lowly soul
He doth himself impart,
And for his dwelling and his throne
Selects the pure in heart."
—*John Keble*

BEHAVIOR IS THE LANGUAGE OF FAITH!

Walk In The Light
Psalm 89

The Psalmist proclaims the heavens, the earth, and the universe are God's creation. The structural components upon which everything rests are: God's righteousness, justice, love, and faithfulness. These inclinations (primitive and current) are uniquely woven into the fabric of human potential.

Individual and communal activities produce superlative results when aligned with these basic building blocks of creation. Cruel and destructive consequences can follow avoidance, misdirection, and misapplication of these impulses thereby provoking the Psalmists' universal cry of exasperation, **"For what vanity have you created mortals?"**

Righteousness, justice, love and faithfulness function as reference points on a compass. Success or failure rests with the navigator, not with the instruments.

"Brightly beams our Father's mercy
From the lighthouse evermore;

But to us he gives the keeping
Of the lights along the shore."
—*Philip Bliss*

BEHAVIOR IS THE LANGUAGE OF FAITH!

Light To Nations
Isaiah 49:1-7

God stirs individuals for a greater purpose than personal rapture. Emphasis upon personal benefit resulting from Sacred Presence is the ultimate arrogance. The Bible tells us about individuals only in the context of their integration as "chosen people" in the Old Testament, or the "body of Christ" in the New Testament. The basic premise upon which the testimony of scripture is based is that humans are formed in the womb to be a blessing, and fulfill the preconceived plan that integrates those created in the *"image of God"* with that which was given them to *"have dominion over and subdue."*

Isaiah's message to the children of Israel was that they erroneously turned their destiny of blessing into a program of exclusive selection and benefit. The New Testament dramatizes implementation of that principle with the temptations of Jesus after his baptism. The Tester concentrates his appeal with repeated references to personal gratification, physical needs, and religious inclinations. These were empty of community benefit. Isaiah and Jesus based their appeal on personal awareness of Sacred Presence that generates a sense of responsibility for the well-being of others. Being a blessing to others is more significant in the Kingdom of God than focusing upon an exclusive franchise.

"O brother man, fold to thy heart thy brother!
Where pity dwells, the peace of God is there;
To worship rightly is to love each other,
Each smile a hymn, each kindly deed a prayer."
—*John Greenleaf Whittier*

BEHAVIOR IS THE LANGUAGE OF FAITH!

Love And Behave
I Thessalonians 4:9-18

The community of faith exists to exemplify love that is taught by God. God's love overcomes estrangement and shares in the creative process. Jesus was the *"exact imprint of God's very being,"* revealing the Kingdom of Heaven on earth. First century Christians impressed their non-Christian contemporaries by imitating Jesus in *"how they loved one another."*

Paul encouraged Christian communities to *"behave properly toward outsiders because forming a cadre of insiders is not the purpose of God's self-revelation."* Outsiders do not know the meaning of the words of faith. Behavior is the language of faith that distinguishes the presence, plan, and purpose of God for creation. Behavior is the message, words provide follow-up for analysis and evaluation.

Validation of faith and behavior relies upon the influential Sacred Presence witnessed by Jesus who *"emptied, humbled, obeyed, and was exalted to the glory of God. (Philippians 2:6-11)"* Weakness resulting in failed performance should not cause despair because followers of Jesus are people of hope who believe that God honors himself by overcoming weakness when it serves his purpose; *"My grace is sufficient for you, for power is made perfect in weakness. (II Corinthians 12:9)"*

228

John Wesley penned one sentence that might help maintain focus in a complex environment: "Simplicity of intention and purity of affection are indeed the wings of the soul."

> "Thou my everlasting portion,
> More than friend or life to me,
> All along my pilgrim journey,
> Savior let me walk with thee."
> — *Fanny J. Crosby*

Dust
Psalm 103

Humility and arrogance are recurring Biblical themes, with arrogance being more frequent. Given this distasteful propensity, why does the Psalmist elegantly emphasize that God forgives, heals, redeems, and loves; is kind, compassionate, just, good, gracious, and slow to anger? Obviously, from the evidence, humanity does not act in a manner that would naturally motivate such a response. Quite unnaturally, human deficiency is the basis for the Psalmists message of hope:

"He knows how we were made; He remembers that we are dust."

God takes into account what we ignore. We are animated dust from beginning to end. He takes our natural condition into consideration and provides us with the opportunity to embrace the breath that blesses life with values and virtues of which dust alone is incapable. Our special gift from God is the capacity to ignore or embrace **"his works and his dominion."** Thanks be to God that he *"remembers we are dust."*

So should we.

"O what blessed hope is ours!
While here on earth we stay.
We more than taste the heavenly powers,
And antedate that day;
We feel the resurrection near,
Our life in Christ concealed,
And with his glorious presence here His life in us revealed."
—*Charles Wesley*

BEHAVIOR IS THE LANGUAGE OF FAITH!

The Glory Of The Lord
Ezekiel 43:1-27

The beautiful imagery Ezekiel uses to describe his experience of God's glorious presence is similar to the vision described in Isaiah 6:1-6. Both emphasize the overwhelming experience of Sacred Presence and their responding sense of humility and unworthiness. Ezekiel said, *"I fell upon my face."* Isaiah said, *"Woe is me! For I am lost; For I am a man of unclean lips..."* There were no petitions or requests for explanations—only awe-struck silence. Ezekiel's prophetic mission was to share the glory of his experience and proclaim to God's chosen people that the glory of the Lord will return to their temple worship when they cease to dishonor his holiness and become *"ashamed."*

We are reminded that religion serves its intended purpose where God is honored by the faith and practice of those who profess loyalty to his Holiness. Otherwise, religion is one among many market-oriented institutions. The Bible represents several thousand years of repetitive history of how people are affected by the presence, or absence, of Sacred Influence in their daily activities. Religion serves its highest and best purpose when God is glorified.

Holy God we praise Thy Name;
Lord of all, we bow before Thee!
All on earth Thy scepter claim,
All in heaven above adore Thee;
Infinite Thy vast domain,
Everlasting is Thy reign.
—*Ignaz Franz*

BEHAVIOR IS THE LANGUAGE OF FAITH!

Against What?
Acts 21:27-36

What motivates people to violence because of something said? The question is especially relevant when the subject is God Who does not need human intervention to establish or maintain His position.

A single word might provide some insight. The word is "our." Temple authorities viewed Paul as one who taught against *"our people, law, and holy place."* They were naturally protective of religious beliefs and traditions that were like braided line attached to an anchor that provided stability in turbulent times. Any effort that appeared to weaken, modify, reattach, or cut the line was vigorously resisted.

When **"words about God"** result in excessive resistance or force, it is not always "about God." It is frequently about a perceived threat to what is *"ours."* The Gospel message teaches that followers of Jesus are called upon to witness to the compelling influence of Sacred Presence. God does not need defending.

231

This is that great thing I know;
This delights and stirs me so:
Faith in him who died to save,
Him who triumphed o'er the grave:
Jesus Christ, the crucified
—*Johann C. Schwedler*

BEHAVIOR IS THE LANGUAGE OF FAITH!

Impressions
II Corinthians 12:1-13

A very good friend once said to me, "You are a big fake. You teach and preach all that Bible stuff and tell about Jesus and how we should love everybody, but I see little of that in you." He was indeed correct. However, I was taken aback because I did not think I projected the image of self-righteousness that obviously affronted him. He wasn't trying to do me a favor by saying what he said. Rather, he was irked. He wasn't angry, but he wanted me to know he wasn't fooled. I am truly grateful to have such a friend.

Hypocrisy is an occupational hazard for religious professionals in that the message is far grander than the messenger. Nonetheless, being a messenger spawns expectations. Having said that, I don't intend to let myself off the hook so easily. I have thought about it a great deal, and I confess that my friend is very perceptive. I, indeed, make the mistake of thinking that religious words have the same weight as good deeds. The irk factor develops in direct proportion to the pretentious persona.

I see a parallel with someone who gives the impression that they are wealthier than they are. It's not that they give a false financial report; but, without actually saying so, they send a

232

wrong message about their wealth. Sooner or later, familiar people realize by evidence that "it just ain't so." God's messengers are similar to pizza delivery people in that value is determined by what they deliver rather than by who delivers it. The Bible displays an odd assortment of individuals who perceive themselves to be God's messengers.

Now, at the end of the day, when I confess to God that my deposit of treasures in the kingdom of heaven shows a negative balance, I impose upon His grace, without expecting passive indulgence, to put my account in balance so I can do business another day and better manage the assets and opportunities He offers while not giving others the impression that my balance is greater than it is. Thankfully, **"God is patient, slow to anger, and abounding in steadfast love"** as He inspires and empowers all people of faith to serve the common good. His message is: **"My grace is sufficient for you, for power is made perfect in weakness."**

Genesis opens with **"In the beginning of creation, God..."** These words are the ballast that gives stability to the process of **"subduing and having dominion over" "Thy will be done on earth as it is in heaven."** Disaster results from rearranging the ballast.

Don's hobby was building small experimental aircraft, having them certified by the appropriate government agency, then selling them. Two years after that sale to the Texan, in which two occupants were killed, he was told that the owner had changed and repositioned the ballast in order to compensate for a grossly obese friend, which caused the plane to become uncontrollable. The first three chapters of Genesis warn mortals about the danger of altered construction that is incompatible with design.

> Thou didst reach forth thy hand and mine enfold;
> I walked and sank not on the storm-vexed sea;
> 'Twas not so much that I on thee took hold,
> As thou, dear Lord, took hold on me.
> —Anonymous

BEHAVIOR IS THE LANGUAGE OF FAITH!

233

What Do We Believe?

I believe in God the Father Almighty, maker of heaven and earth; And in Jesus Christ his only Son our Lord who was conceived by the Holy Spirit, born of the Virgin Mary, suffered under Pontius Pilate, was crucified, dead, and buried; the third day he rose from the dead; he ascended into heaven, and sitteth at the right hand of God the Father Almighty; from thence he shall come to judge the quick and the dead.

I believe in the Holy Spirit, the holy catholic Church, the communion of saints, the forgiveness of sins, the resurrection of the body, and the life everlasting. Amen.

LOVE- "To love is to act intentionally, in sympathetic response to others (including God), to promote overall well-being."[1]

Love, The Greatest Gift and Way.

"If I speak in the tongues of mortals and angels, but do not have love, I am a noisy gong or a clanging cymbal. And If I have prophetic powers, and understand all mysteries and all knowledge, and if I have all faith, so as to remove mountains, but do not have love, I am nothing If I give away all my possessions, and if I hand over my body so that I may boast, but do not have love, I am nothing.

Love is patient; love is kind; love is not envious or boastful or arrogant or rude. It does not insist on its own way; it is not irritable or resentful, it does not rejoice in wrongdoing, but rejoices in truth. It bears all things, believes all things; hopes all things, endures all things.

Love never ends." (I Corinthians 13:1-8)

---

[1] Defining Love-A Philosophical, Scientific, and Theological Engagement. By Thomas Jay Oord

How Shall We Behave?

Jesus said: "You shall love the Lord your God with all your heart, and with all your soul, and with all your mind, and with all your strength. The second is this. You shall love your neighbor as yourself."

- Love your enemies.
- Do good to those who hate you.
- Bless those who curse you.
- Pray for those who abuse you.
- If anyone strikes you on the cheek, offer the other also.
- And from everyone who takes your coat, do not even withhold your shirt.
- Give to everyone who begs from you.
- If anyone takes away your goods, do not ask for them again.
- Do to others as you would have them do to you.
- Be merciful, just as your Father is merciful.
- Do not judge.
- Do not condemn.
- Forgive; the measure you give will be the measure you get back.

"I am sending you out like sheep in the midst of wolves, so be wise as serpents and innocent as doves."

"Not everyone who says to me, 'Lord, Lord,' will enter the kingdom of heaven, but only the one who does the will of my Father in heaven."

BEHAVIOR IS THE LANGUAGE OF FAITH

"The Holy Spirit, whom the Father will send in my name, ...will remind you of everything I have said to you." John 14:26

Scripture Index

51495

McBryde Publishing
NEW BERN NORTH CAROLINA USA

9 781733 982405

www.ingramcontent.com/pod-product-compliance
Lightning Source LLC
Chambersburg PA
CBHW031510040426
42445CB00009B/161